A JOURNEY TO

Engaged Philanthropy

A JOURNEY TO

Engaged
Philanthropy

TIM McCARTHY

For information contact:
Empty Abundance
9325 Progress Parkway
Mentor, OH 44060
1.877.352.4420

ISBN paperback: 978-0-9907481-0-6
ISBN eBook: 978-0-9907481-1-3

PCN: Library of Congress Control Number: 2014949532

Cover design by Don Iannone
Interior design by Dotti Albertine

To my mother Margaret Mary McDonough McCarthy,
a journalist at the *Chicago Tribune* during its heyday
in the 1930s and 1940s. I once asked Mom, "How can I
become a good writer?" She answered, "Write."

This is for you, Mom.

And to Michael Levin and Sara Stratton of
www.businessghost.com, who have been my patient coaches
through the two years it took to write this book.
Without their outline, heavy editing, and guidance,
this book would be unreadable.

To learn more about Tim McCarthy's philanthropic work and his foundation, The Business of Good, please visit online:

www.TheBusinessofGood.org

CONTENTS

After spending 15 years as the director of a charitable foundation distributing millions of dollars in grants, I discovered that I was doing it all wrong.

Like most of my peers, I was diligently following a model of American philanthropy that you might call *We Want to Help You.* The trouble is, "The poor you will always have with you" (Mark 14:7). Why? Because, inadvertently, traditional charity often keeps in place the very problems it works so hard to eliminate. How? Like opioids, organizations can become dependent on regular grants and suffer or die if they are withdrawn.

A scary thought: what would happen to the 401(k)s of millions of nonprofit and foundation workers if the difficulties they combat were to be largely solved or even eliminated? What would become of the grand edifice of Big Charity?

Most foundations operate in silos, faithfully pursuing their "mission," "focus areas" or "vision." While these articles of faith may be laudable, the Lone Ranger mentality ignores many possibilities. 1) Other foundations and corporations might want to collaborate with them, leveraging their impact. 2) Individuals just awakening to the charitable ethic might be ready to join in writing checks or providing other volunteer services to donee organizations. 3) Foundation program officers could assume a new role as coaches, becoming partners with nonprofit grantees in carrying out their initiatives based on business disciplines. 4) Nurturing social enterprises— those hybrid start-ups that serve the commonweal while maintaining a positive cash flow—might be a good investment of foundation grant dollars. 5) Nonprofits that funnel foundation grants to "the poor" might be willing to accept some measure of responsibility for their own financial self-sufficiency by developing sources of program-related income, making them less dependent on endless grants.

All this did not strike me as a sudden epiphany.

It started to arrive during my first lunch with Tim McCarthy, author of this book and founder of the Business of Good Foundation. That conversation created a queasy *uh-oh!* moment that prodded me to re-examine my philanthropic orthodoxy. It made me recall my corporate years in commercial banking and its steely-eyed focus on rigorous and pragmatic business plans. Could the nonprofits that receive our grants benefit by adopting similar measurable and accountable practices?

Before long, Tim and I were making collaborative grants to organizations we had carefully vetted, making sure that they were open to coaching, willing to commit to metrics and deliverables, and ready to begin weaning themselves off the bottle of routine charitable contributions.

Of course, this approach to philanthropy did not come to Tim as a sudden revelation either.

That's what this book is about—his gradual awakening to perfecting the mechanics of "giving with an open hand." Warts-and-all stories of success and failure. Personal handicaps, shortcomings and disappointments. Life experiences full of joy and pain, along with those of his heroes, friends and readers. It was out this often-messy cauldron of hard knocks that a new paradigm of engaged philanthropy emerged.

"I'm no more or less qualified than anyone else to do this," Tim says. "In fact, it is by putting my losses and my gains under the harsh light of publication that I hope to be helpful."

He believes that there are millions of Tim McCarthys out there: people who are doing well—or are on their way to doing well—materially, but are still looking for more from life. In speaking engagements around the country he has explained his new model of business-based, engaged philanthropy to hundreds of CEOs and highly successful entrepreneurs—people who may have been totally consumed in achieving financial success but are now wondering what to do with it. After hearing him speak, 85% of these leaders said they were ready to give more to charity.

A final clue to who Tim McCarthy is? He dedicates this book to the many people in need who will be served by the donation of 100% of the proceeds from its sale.

ROBERT MILLER
Author of *Getting to Know My Self*

CHAPTER 1

The Liquidity Event

MY UNIQUENESS IS the same as everyone else's: it is a product of how I arrived at this place in time.

I was fired from a C-level job at thirty-four years old, had the assets of my business frozen at forty-three, and then became extraordinarily wealthy at fifty-four from a transaction that occurred in one day.

To invite you more fully into my world, I'll start by sharing some details from that one great day. I'll also tell you about the day I was fired and the day my assets were frozen—the two worst days of my business career. By zooming in on just these three eventful days, you'll gain a clearer understanding of my personal choices in the pursuit of happiness.

May 14, 2007

At noon, a limousine dropped us off at Molinari's, the finest restaurant in Mentor, Ohio, the home base of the company we'd started nineteen years earlier. The restaurant was closed for our private celebration.

We hugged and high-fived our sixty-five fellow workers who had built the business we were selling. After drinks and a lovely lunch, I told them that they were the survivors of two or three hundred people who had "come and gone" during our nineteen years in business.

Each person at our goodbye lunch had a story, from Patricia White, our CEO, to Philip Griesmer, one of our assembly line workers.

Patricia White had been a volunteer for the Junior Service League when we met. She came to work on the phones with several of my wife Alice's JSL friends and after a while said to me, "I'm going back into the workforce now that my kids are mostly grown up, and I'm not sure I want to go back to teaching school."

"Well," I said, "just take a job in operations here and then you can reevaluate once a year, and decide to go back to school if you don't like it."

That was seventeen years ago, and most years she came to me to say, "I don't think I'm going to teach this year."

Pat was the very soul of the company because she was

brilliant, yet entirely uncomplicated. By the way she kept things simple, she taught me about patience and winning.

My favorite Pat story begins when our largest client, Goodyear, which provided a little over 25 percent of our total revenue in 1997, informed us they were taking our work in-house. I reacted with great anger. I told the client they were crazy to think they could do our work themselves and that they would deeply regret firing us.

A few months later, as we neared the end of the transfer of our work, Pat came to me and said, "Tim, they want us to keep one small piece of business—about $25,000 a year of work they are unable to do. I've told them yes."

I remember screaming, "Bullshit! Let them learn how to do it themselves; they're the ones walking away. Who cares if they screw it up?"

And Pat said, "I do. And I want my nose under their tepee in case they do screw it up. Maybe then they will come back to us since we'll have shown our loyalty to them. Let's take the high ground here."

Indeed, less than nine months later, Pat walked into my office and said, "It worked, Tim. Goodyear is bringing their entire business back to us."

Pat eventually became CEO of our company.

Phillip Griesmer was on the lowest tier of our company, and just as Pat did, he became a symbol of what we stood for.

They both taught me about playing with the cards you've been dealt.

Goodyear gave us a lousy hand in business, and Pat fixed it. Phil worked with a lousy hand that life dealt.

The deacon at our church asked me in 1996 if we had any jobs that could be done by an autistic person who had just lost both of his parents and whose uncle was trying to help him live independently.

Phil came for a two-week trial on our coupon "assembly line" and was still with us eleven years later on that day in 2007. Things didn't always go smoothly. Our Director of Operations said Phil was slow compared to the rest of the workers, but unlike the others, Phil rarely made a mistake. That was Phil's business value to the company.

More valuable was the perspective he gave everyone in our company. At lunch, or in any social setting, Phil was uncomfortable. A slender man with coke-bottle glasses, Phil would lean away from you if you came anywhere near him. If you spoke to him, he would turn his head away from you, but over time would kind of sigh, almost mew in response. I never had a moment with Phil that felt comfortable.

Every day, rain or shine, cold or hot, Phil rode his bicycle to our building, about six miles from his apartment in the next town. And when a company event was happening, he would wait in the doorway of my office until I noticed him. After much prompting, he would mumble, "Can you give me a ride?" Alice and I learned to enjoy taking him to parties and challenging ourselves to get him to talk.

One day at our monthly company meeting, I noted Phil's contributions to our company and his inspiring presence among us, and the place broke out into thunderous applause. Swaying back and forth and looking like he was lost, I noticed a lovely grin on his face and a tear in Phil's eye while we were cheering for him.

That's perspective: Phil's version of an abundant life despite overwhelming physical and neurological challenges.

I was glad to have both Phil and Pat among those gathered at our goodbye lunch on the day we sold the business, representing the hard work that had gone into the company. I told them and all others gathered that I was proud to have conceived the business and gotten through the early years, but that it was them who had brought us today's remarkable accomplishment. As the drivers of our success, they each would receive two years' pay as my thanks, the first check of which was in an envelope to be handed out as they left the luncheon.

After tearful goodbyes, our management team, my family, and our new friend from the private equity firm that was buying us piled back into the limousine and headed for downtown

Cleveland. On the ride, I suddenly found my mind drifting back to a very different day, a dark day twelve years ago, when the company we were selling almost went out of business.

June 15, 1995

I knew we were facing financial challenges as a few months before we had invested heavily in the introduction of a new product, but the call from our banker still took me off guard. After all, we'd just been named to the Inc. 500—*Inc.* magazine's list of the fastest growing private firms in the United States.

"Tim, I have bad news," said Jim, our third bank rep in just over a year. "Our loan committee decided this morning that your company has put itself too much at risk, and we are going to move to freeze your assets."

I said, "I'll call you back." I ran down to the office of our new CFO, Jack Zaback, and asked him what "freeze our assets" meant.

"The short answer," Jack said, "is we will be out of business."

"Can they do that?" I asked Jack. I was clearly in shock.

"They can," he said. "And it appears they are going to."

For the first time since my dad died five years earlier, I cried. But after a few minutes, I realized if we didn't figure something out quickly, we were going to be the only Inc. 500 company that went out of business before getting the award.

So, once I pulled myself together, I called my big brother,

Miller. As the call proceeded, I started wondering if he regretted taking my call. My anxiety was incredibly high, so I probably sounded like a ten-year-old who'd had his lunchbox stolen by the class bully. But Miller had always been patient with me in business. I could also tell he was listening and processing while I was talking.

Finally, Miller said, "The bank has already committed to putting you down, so you can't change their mind politely. If it were me, I would call the highest person you can get to at the bank and invite them to look at your books. More importantly, let him know that if they don't come out to look at your books, you will sue them for tortious interference the day you receive the formal asset freeze order."

I hung up and immediately called an attorney friend to find out if there was such a thing as tortious interference and if I had the grounds to make such a threat. He confirmed the strategy, so I called my banker back and said, "Please find your boss's boss's boss and tell them they should call me quickly or my attorney will be in their office tomorrow morning."

And sure enough, the senior vice president of commercial lending called me about fifteen minutes later. His name was Bill.

"Bill," I said, "do you know anything about my business and the action your bank decided to take against me today?"

"Yes, Tim, I was in the meeting when we made the decision."

"I think you may want to come out here and go through our books before you take that action."

"Why?"

"Because I haven't broken any covenants with you, and so if you proceed with freezing our assets without looking more closely, I will be able to prove to a court that you put me out of business without cause. The charge will be tortious interference."

After hours of threats and counter threats, the bank agreed to send auditors out immediately to check out our books, and Jack agreed to stay all night if necessary to show them every financial document in our files.

The next day, my banker called me back and said, "Everything checked out, but my boss is really mad. If you'll agree to get a new bank within thirty days, we'll agree to leave you alone until then."

I wanted to scream, "With friends like you, who needs enemies?" Instead, I quietly hung up and started calling friends for bank references. Only two weeks later, we secured the bank with which we still do business today.

After the search began for bankers, I also cancelled my trip to the Inc. 500 conference. There was no way I was going to enjoy celebrating after that brush with death.

And I had too much work to do.

It was the most jarring episode I'd experienced since I was fired eight years before.

December 22, 1987

The CEO of a large restaurant chain called me into his office.

It had been a tough but fascinating year. In April, I had become his chief marketing officer. Moving Alice and our three young children (ages eight, seven, and four) to a new town was difficult, but at thirty-four, I controlled $50 million in marketing, sales, and product development for 650 restaurants and was paid more than $150,000 for what I considered to be that privilege.

I sat on the company's executive committee and occupied a huge office in a lavish modern office building on the grounds of the airport in Dayton, Ohio. And while we missed our friends, we'd bought a lovely home in a beautiful little farm town called Troy, just north of Dayton. The house was larger than anything we'd dreamed of, and the neighborhood was such a lovely combination of luxury and farm life that Alice could walk the children to their horse-riding lessons. We were the consummate young urban professionals: yuppies.

But at the company, it was chaos. A New York hedge-fund guy named Asher Edelman had just bought us out, and we had a lot to prove due to the debt taken on in his leveraged buyout.

And yet we seemed to be making progress; in fact, we'd had record sales as we headed toward the end of that year.

Shortly after I arrived to the office of Frank, the CEO, he informed me that I was fired.

"We're being bought out again," he said. He went on to explain that this time, the buyer was an even more famous hedge fund guy named John Kluge and that his folks had their own marketing person.

"In fact," Frank stated, "he's been working for a couple months as a consultant already."

He told me there was a policeman at his door who would escort me out of the building and that I could return after hours to pick up my personal belongings.

As I left Frank's office, I remember feeling as if I'd been in a car accident. Shock set in. It was ten in the morning. I called home but there was no answer. Alice had surely already started her daily taxi service getting the kids here and there. So I drove around aimlessly trying to decide what to do.

Being 100 percent Irish, the few times I'd ever thought about what I'd do if I got fired, I figured I'd head for a bar to drown my sorrows. But I didn't. My car passed by the public library and it seemed as good a place as any to sort things out. I parked the car, headed into the stacks, and sat trembling and staring into space for more than an hour trying to understand what had happened and how it would affect my life.

I went through every question, from "How do I tell Alice that our family has no income as of today?" to "Why didn't I see this coming?"

I broke into a cold sweat when I realized that though I was making so much money ($150,000 is equivalent to $310,000 today), we had not saved one dime. Sweet Lord, I was doomed.

After about two hours of my own version of the Garden of Gethsemane (praying, pleading, agonizing), I started writing lists.

The first list I wrote was of the things I'd done wrong that year. It was a long list as I was young and impetuous and had taken way more risks than were necessary. Convinced of my rightness, I had lost business friends to disagreements. When I looked over the list I realized I had opened myself up to justifiable scrutiny.

Then, I wrote a list of things I wanted to do in my life, none of which was starting a business. Later that day, I arrived home to the unexpected pleasure of kids who couldn't care less what I did for a living and a wife who simply said, "We'll get through this."

After dinner, I asked the boys if they wanted to go with me to clear out my office and they did. While I tearfully put things in boxes, they giggled outside my office door as they made and threw easel pad–sized paper airplanes off the third-floor balcony into the lobby below. I don't remember a time I wanted to control my kids less!

Sweet perspective, thy name is children.

May 14, 2007

Lola—our next stop on the day we sold the business—makes a great martini. Again, we were driven there by limousine, and once inside, we stood at a bar that glowed orange from within, clinking our celebratory martinis. All that was left to do was wait for my cell phone to ring with the news that the buyer's electronic transfer of $45 million had cleared our account. I nursed my drink, laughing at anything and everything the private-equity guy muttered. He was paying the bill, after all.

Then my cell phone rang. Everyone heard it and stopped.

It was our banker, who would soon leave to join us in celebration.

"Tim, the money has successfully transferred to your checking account."

Wife, daughter, son, senior managers, and our new private-equity friends all hugged and howled.

Our destination had been reached. The eight senior managers present would receive 18 percent of the stock in the new company, and my family now had a fortune that we wouldn't have dared to dream that we'd own. The fields we had planted with hundred-hour workweeks and good hiring and coaching were harvested.

It was over.

Only I knew, instinctively, that it was not.

It seemed we'd reached the ultimate summit after a lifetime of peaks and valleys.

On May 15, 2007, I went back down into the valley.

CHAPTER 2

Anhedonia

The mass of men lead lives of quiet desperation. What
is called resignation is confirmed desperation. From
the desperate city you go into the desperate country,
and have to console yourself with the bravery of minks
and muskrats. A stereotyped but unconscious despair
is concealed even under what are called the games and
amusements of mankind. There is no play in them, for
this comes after work. But it is a characteristic of wisdom
not to do desperate things.

—Henry David Thoreau, *Walden*

IT IS SUCH a strange word: *anhedonia*. I asked a friend what it
meant. "It is," he said, "the emptiness or the lack of pleasure
that is derived from material things or stimuli outside of ourselves usually found joyful."

The Pot and the Kettle

I know about anhedonia because there was a time when I could have been its poster child.

Anhedonia apparently comes in many forms, and mine is medically diagnosed as dysthymia. My anhedonia is a lower-intensity but longer-lasting form of depression. Most clinically depressed people have episodes during which their depression comes to a strong head—they can't get out of bed, they can't face anyone, and they can't get anything done.

A person with dysthymia can have a similar experience, but it tends to be in a less intense form that can last for years. It never becomes acute, or something that keeps you from getting out of bed, but it seems to grab on and take hold of your soul. When my dysthymia was at its worst, I dreaded going to parties and other activities I normally took great pleasure in—things like reading a good book, playing my guitar, or working out.

For years I thought my dysthymia was just my Irish nature: "chronic melancholy." And also, like so many of my Irish brethren, my bouts were interspersed with buoyant, happier periods. When not depressed, I can be the life of the party, read with spirited interest, and play and sing with all my heart and soul.

And I can also get overtaken by stress and striving.

I've always had a type A (Alice says, "type AAA") personality. I remember as a kid I sometimes felt like I would come out of my skin. When my feet hit the floor in the morning, I was off and running. In high school, I made it a goal to play every sport, act in school plays, and get into school politics—all of this while I was also working part-time after-school and summer jobs.

In college, my hot engine was somewhat sated in the first two years by drugs and alcohol, which masked a lengthy bout of depression. I had funded those first two years with my summer job as a shoeshine boy at the local country club, and so I had a little too much time on my hands during the school year. I filled the empty spaces with partying and came perilously close to dropping out.

In 1972, my savings ran out during the final quarter of my sophomore year. That seemed to shake me out of that particular depressive episode, and I proceeded to sprint toward my degree by working for two quarters, then going to school for two quarters, until I graduated in March of 1975. My jobs were managing campaigns and doing legislative work in the Ohio Senate, and my degree was a BA in political science, so I was running at one hundred miles per hour again, and my focus sharpened considerably.

Later in 1975, I married Alice and became the executive director of a party organization in Michigan for four years. Running seventy local candidates every two years while supporting state and national campaigns in our county made for eighty-hour workweeks—and I liked it.

In 1979, I switched to the advertising business, and by 1987 I had risen from an entry-level job to senior vice president, group supervisor of a major Madison Avenue–based advertising agency. This was accomplished through my ambitious and curious nature and workweeks similar to those I kept in politics. We had three beautiful children and went through a succession of lovely houses and cars.

During those years, each victory—each higher salary, award-winning campaign, bonus, or promotion—was followed quickly by my setting a new, higher goal (i.e., more was never enough).

After losing my job in late 1987, I went into business for myself the following year. As anyone who has bootstrapped a business will tell you, the first five years were murderous.

By the time I was forty, my ambition started to affect my health. Relatively speaking, I was in good shape. I was always slightly over my ideal weight, but I was a nonsmoker who ran two to four miles every other day and followed a reasonably thoughtful diet. Still, I found myself short of breath, and I began to experience heart palpitations.

I was experiencing what seemed like heart attacks. And so I went to my family doctor and he began a series of tests. Each test came back negative. And yet I became increasingly worried because these "attacks" became more frequent.

One time, while driving to a local appointment, I became

so lightheaded and dizzy that I pulled over to the side of the road and called the doctor. Since they had exhausted all other tests, he said, "Okay, that's it," and scheduled a heart catheterization for me.

I was referred to a specialist, Dr. Sam Wilson. As the camera was casually injected into my femoral artery, we began chatting, and he showed me how to watch on the screen as the camera moved through my arteries.

When the first real picture came up, he said, "Wow, look at that—no plaque anywhere."

Then later: "There's an artery I'd like to call my own—it's so clear."

Finally I said, "Sam, are you saying there are no problems with my heart or anything around it?"

"Yes," Sam responded. "In fact, I'm telling you that you have the plumbing of a young horse."

"So, am I a hypochondriac? Is that why I am having these attacks?"

"Actually, no," he said. "What I think is that no one in the world, including me, respects the physical outcomes of stress. If you ask me, we all live in nineteenth-century bodies while we're moving at a twenty-first-century pace."

In short, I was a successful businessman with a beautiful wife and kids, a lovely home, two cars, lots of friends, a fulfilling career . . . and I was making myself sick.

A few days later I went back to my internist and said, "So, now what do I do?"

"Only one doctor left for us to visit, Tim," he told me. "The psychiatrist."

That actually made my heart stop again.

Upset, I somewhat hesitantly said, "But, Doc, I don't believe in psychiatry."

"You better start believing in it," he said, "because there is nothing else I can do for you."

About six months and three brain-mechanics later, I believed. My stay in psychotherapy lasted over two years and I still go back and get my oil checked once or twice a year.

At one point during my therapy, the doctor asked me to refrain from drinking any alcohol. I said, "Fine, for how long?" and she said, "I'll let you know." Every couple sessions after that she would ask me if I'd imbibed and after about five months of "no" answers, she said "I did that to make sure your system was drug-free," and then proceeded to prescribe an anti-depressant medication for me to ingest daily, specifically Citalopram.

Taking medication for my dysthymia was even more difficult for me than submitting to therapy in the first place. I felt weak at best, abnormal at worst, but I figured I'd run out of options, and so I would try it for a few months to see if it helped me overcome my bouts with depression and panic. That was many years ago.

The combination of psychotherapy and drug therapy has changed my life for the better. Under professional care, I've added many skill-building techniques for dealing with dysthymia, including meditation, exercise, sleep, good diet, reading, writing, and playing music. I also learned I was a successful businessman with a beautiful wife and kids, a lovely home, two cars, lots of friends, and a fulfilling career, a.k.a.: *perspective.*

It Only Hurts When I Don't Laugh

As I've recognized and modified my own behaviors, I have noticed more frequently that many of my friends seem to also be affected by anhedonia. Some hop from one thing to another—purchasing a new house (or a second or third house), getting a new boat, a new motorcycle, then capping a week of obtaining new possessions with a whiskey bender. That says to me that the experience of purchasing a new home or expensive toy was fleeting fulfillment—the joy dissipated by the weekend.

Many other anhedonians, in the great Judeo-Christian tradition, hover between feeling grateful and guilty. One friend recently wrote, "I'm so happy that I am safe and warm and have enough food to eat when two of six billion people on the planet make less than two dollars a day, and sad because I wonder why I should be so lucky and they so unfortunate."

Is my friend happy or sad? It's not clear to me.

"Money doesn't buy happiness" is an enduring maxim

because it's true. A few studies also support the disconnection between accumulating wealth with happiness and meaning. Recent Gallup poll data shows that residents of the United States are three times richer than they were in 1950, but the happiness ratings haven't shifted.

A 2010 Princeton study found that life satisfaction rises with income, but that everyday happiness—another measure of well-being—changes little once a person reaches $75,000 a year. Another Gallup survey, conducted in 132 countries, found what we might expect: that people in wealthy countries rate higher in happiness than those in poor countries. However, 95 percent of those surveyed in poverty-stricken countries such as Ethiopia, Kyrgyzstan, and Sierra Leone reported leading meaningful lives, while less than 60 percent reported such a feeling in wealthier countries such as ours.

Another widely published survey by psychologist Roy Baumeister suggested that "happiness, or immediate fulfillment, is largely irrelevant to meaningfulness." In other words, so many who finally achieve financial excess are unfulfilled by the rewards presented to them.

One of my readers said, "I had wealth once; lost it all. My life didn't change all that much. In fact one could argue that it has changed for the better. I have fun with what I do now because I have purpose."

My friend Pete Accorti said it even more simply: "Money is usually not a factor in doing the things I want to do the most."

My own experience reflects the same phenomenon.

When I graduated from college, I aimed to make $40,000 a year by the time I was forty and yet I achieved it before age thirty. By fifty-five, I wanted to be on the board of a NYSE company—I achieved that status when I was thirty-four years old. By forty-four, my start-up company was a financial and creative success, and by fifty-five, I was retired.

And yet during many of those same years I could not find fulfillment. I suffered from anhedonia. This leads me to believe that money did not bring me happiness, especially as it pertains to meaningfulness and personal fulfillment.

Those with excess income, whether it be from winning the lottery or making $150,000 a year when previously $75,000 was enough, find themselves using that money to search for fulfillment that never arrives. And yet, they try again and again and again . . .

It also seems ironic that wealth building amplifies stress and increases, rather than reduces, anxiety. When our financial plans go well, we still worry endlessly that circumstances will change soon through recession, a lost job, a divorce, illness, or business failure. That is, even when we're materially satisfied, we seem to be expecting our luck to change.

Take, for example, a reader of mine. He has millions of dollars in the bank and told me he is not sure that will be enough. "I constantly wonder what will happen if we have another major recession."

No matter how much we save, we wonder about unforeseen emergencies. We wonder what might happen. We see a sad story in the media as a warning, and then imagine it happening to us. It's the great American pastime known as "disasterizing." And before I realized there was little I could do to change unforeseeable circumstances, I did quite a bit of disasterizing.

Empty Abundance Yields Only Abundant Emptiness

To a certain extent, we've all experienced the phenomenon of wanting more—thinking the next career advancement, the next consumer item, the next relationship will be the one to make us feel whole . . . only to find that we quickly return to a state of wanting. Part of this is just the human condition. But when we live in the land of plenty, this drive for more, more, more to fill an empty space makes us lose track of what we already have. Worse, it can become a pathology that poisons relationships and limits or outright crushes joy.

To give a stark example, here's a true story about a billionaire I used to know pretty well.

While sailing the Mediterranean on a colleague's exquisite

hundred-foot yacht, my friend called his business manager to excitedly describe everything about the magnificent yacht he was travelling on. At the end of the call, my friend told his manager, "We have to acquire one of these."

After taking a few moments to collect himself, the manager said to my friend, "Jack, you bought that exact boat four years ago, and it's currently docked unused in Miami."

The "Non-Anhedonians"

Take a moment to consider the "non-anhedonians" we know. They're more fun to watch than the anhedonians. These joyful folks come in many forms, and they are everywhere, every day. For me, they include the following:

> ❯ A teacher I know who also volunteers at Bible school on Sundays. (Shouldn't she be tired of kids by the end of the week?)
> ❯ My young executive friend now making $150,000 who sits on a volunteer board that requires she invest five hours a week and significant money to their cause.
> ❯ Alice's friend, Debbie, who has a very busy house-cleaning business and yet also provides overnight home care for elderly people, often for no pay.

These three people ironically strike me as among the happiest people I know, while my anhedonian friends seem to chase their tails.

So, how is it that I feel so unsatisfied? What causes the emptiness in my soul that drives my ambition, my continual striving?

A verse from Don Henley's song "Heart of the Matter" comes to mind:

What are these voices outside love's open door
Make us throw off our contentment
And beg for something more?

The only answer I can come up with—and it forms the core of this book and my life's learning to date—is that I must "come to the moment." These are the moments when I can see what's right in front of me: the good, the bad, the happy, and the sad. Only then can I deal with things as they truly are.

No addiction to the sadness, no grasping for the happiness. No clinging to the good or bad moments. Just seeing them as they are and experiencing them—then letting them go.

Over time, I have found that the cure for anhedonia, at least for me, is service. Of equal importance is my work to become present in this moment. This moment, this time, this life—that's all we have, since there will be no other.

CHAPTER 3

Abundant Addictions

God, grant me the serenity to accept the things I cannot change, The courage to change the things I can, And the wisdom to know the difference.
—Serenity Prayer

HAND IN HAND with anhedonia is another nationwide affliction: addiction. We are more familiar with the phenomenon of addiction than with that of anhedonia, but it might be that addiction is merely a symptom, while anhedonia is the root cause.

Just as my life has been touched by anhedonia, I've also skated the surface of addiction—and not solely the kind of addiction we think of first: substance addiction. We fill the emptiness in our lives with any number of pleasures, and whether these pleasures are chemical or otherwise, they can still become "too much of a good thing." Since my liquidity event, various kinds of pleasures are now available to me 24–7, but my conscious choice is to utilize these privileges rarely enough that I thoroughly enjoy them.

I've never been shy about games and amusements. For me, though, their rarity heightens their appeal. Said another way, everything about our lives is fleeting, or as the Buddha teaches, "impermanent." And games and amusements are the most impermanent of all.

I've enjoyed sports such as skiing, boating, and golf in the finest places; attended the biggest professional sporting events; and I've been amused in such spectacular venues as the Cayman Islands and the Amalfi Coast of Italy. I have consumed fine wines, liquors, and champagnes; smoked the finest cigars; and I've eaten the finest meals in spectacular locations.

I've never considered myself "safe" from addiction. And so while earlier in my life, financial constraints kept me from becoming addicted to what I consider to be life's more engaging amusements, I now choose to self-impose limits.

Currently, I'm on a budget with craft beer because I worry that I enjoy it too much. If it became an everyday thing, I worry that I would become addicted to it. And given my ancestors and family's proclivities, that's probably a healthy worry.

Am I into self-denial? No, but it seems the more of "the good life" I have, the less I seem to enjoy each instance. I recall a cigarette ad from my childhood: "Are you smoking more and enjoying it less? Try Tareyton." Until my daughter, Caitlin, was born in my thirty-second year, I smoked up to three packs of cigarettes a day and I enjoyed it less and less over time.

Addiction seems pandemic in the United States. Infections such as alcohol, sex, drugs, cell phones, gambling, Internet games, fantasy sports, and shopping make it appear that we are driven by our distractions. In fact, if we are not sufficiently distracted, we create distractions from our distractions.

I'm no preacher, since drugs are the only item on this list I abstain from. In fact, I'm known to surf the Internet while listening to a ball game while eating and talking on the phone. And this is when I'm driving my car!

How Do I Love Thee? Let Me Count the Addictions

Here is my typical day: I wake sleepy but always glad to see another day. I stumble to the coffeemaker and get that going while also preparing the cat's breakfast (never thought I'd see the day I admitted that). I go to the front door to pick up the morning newspapers, which I bring back up the stairs to sit down and read slowly while I drink several cups of coffee over a span of no less than forty-five minutes.

I then head upstairs to my office and crank up the computer. I first respond to any emails that came in overnight. I then attack the emails that came in late in the day before and ones I've saved to remind me of work I've promised to do. About an hour into that, I make my daily to-do list.

When I leave my office, my nose is immediately in my

iPhone, where it remains most of the day no matter where I am. I consume at least one (often two) Diet Cokes during my day. During meetings, I keep my computer open (if I can) even while others are talking.

By the end of the day, no earlier than five and no later than seven, I turn to one to three glasses of beer to offset the one to three cups of coffee I started my day with. At night I'm either in a restaurant with friends or businesspeople, or on the couch playing games on my computer while watching TV with my wife—and in either case, I eat four or five courses. And I never go to bed without something sweet—these days usually a Weight Watchers ice cream bar.

I hit the bed with my Nook because I've convinced myself over the years that I cannot go to sleep without a book in my hand. This addiction is so bad that if I've forgotten my Nook or a book when I'm away, I will search the hotel or even drive off in the night to find something to read.

So, maybe I'd like to think of myself as not addicted to anything, and yet I've counted eight things that I find it hard to imagine a day without. Coffee and beer are particularly troublesome to me ever since the local roasting and craft brewing movements. I can no longer have a regular cup of either brew. Instead I search any chance I get for the dark, hoppy local ones.

My computers and iPhone make me feel like an anxious but friendly dog following the mail carrier all day saying,

"Have you got anything for me yet?" My Diet Cokes and sweet treats have zero nutritional value. And I am not only addicted to reading on my Nook; I am also addicted to mindless mysteries.

And the grandest addiction of all for me—and I'm not alone—is anxiety. My racing mind starts the moment I wake, even in the middle of the night, and lasts until I go back to sleep.

The clinical term for this dysfunction is rumination, which means excessive self-reflection and a preoccupation with both past and current negative experiences. My mother called worry her "rocking chair," since it gave her lots of motion but it never got her anywhere. Buddhists call American rumination "monkey mind," as we who are addicted simply swing from branch to branch, always finding fault and stressing about one worry and then quickly moving onto the next branch/worry.

Whatever it's called, it haunts me.

One Trillion Dollars of Addiction

It appears I'm not alone. Here's what Americans spent in 2011 on my particular addictions:

> Coffee: $20 *billion* . . . that's billion with a *b*
> Cell phone data charges: $100 billion
> Beer: $210 billion
> Restaurants: $406 billion

Now that's just the consumer spending. Another $140 billion was spent in 2011 advertising these products to us.

And for those who couldn't control their addictions, the 2011 bill included another $400 billion just on obesity and alcohol recovery programs.

I refuse to "rail against the machine" in a general sense. It is what it is, as the kids now say. Instead I simply believe it's important for me to better understand what role pleasure should hold in my life. That is, how do my addictions effect me personally?

If I didn't fear addiction, I'd buy a combination brewpub and coffee shop. Sadly, I'm sure that instead of making me happier, it would more likely fulfill my dad's prediction that if he ever bought a bar, he might become his "own best customer."

So, tinkering with quotas on the things that could become addictions remains important to me.

One time thirty years ago, I rode in a golf cart with a very wealthy older man who told me, "I've drank pretty freely all my life and it occurred to me recently that I can't think of one single positive outcome alcohol ever had on me."

That really struck me. His irrefutable logic was, "If I'm seeking to be happier, why do something so frequently that doesn't make me happier?"

He, along with others, has convinced me that restaurants,

craft beer, and specialty coffee serve me better the less, not the more, I enjoy them.

It's actually embarrassing to write this chapter, admitting to how much I cling to so many things. I imagine that most of us cling to these or similar things; things that, in many cases, can detract from our health, let alone our happiness.

And since nothing in abundance will make me any happier, why bother?

Money Crimes

Sociologist Phil Slater coined the term "wealth addiction" in a book by the same name. Although he wrote his book thirty years ago, Slater's term pinpoints a crisis that we still face today, and that is growing. We can find examples of wealth addiction everywhere in American culture. Wall Street is perhaps our most glaring example, especially after the crash of recent years. Take, for example, former Wall Street banker, Sam Polk, who confessed in a *New York Times* op-ed, "In my last year on Wall Street, my bonus was $3.6 million—and I was angry because it wasn't big enough. I was thirty years old, had no children to raise, no debts to pay, no philanthropic goal in mind. I wanted more money for exactly the same reason an alcoholic needs another drink: I was addicted."

But wealth addiction is older than Slater's book. It has

pervaded American culture perhaps even from the beginning. One of America's greatest writers and humorists, Mark Twain, wrote over a century ago, "Nothing incites to money-crimes like great poverty or great wealth." Samuel Clemens—Twain's real name—was writing from a place of personal experience, having both built and lost a fortune. But it would appear that he overcame his addiction to money, for although he filed for bankruptcy in the mid-1890s, he later chose to pay all his pre-bankruptcy creditors in full despite not being legally required to do so.

What is it in American culture that drives the accumulation of wealth to the point of addiction? Wealth addicts I've known—and even more often, their apologists—argue that by amassing great fortunes, they benefit everyone. This is often called the "trickle-down" theory. Titans of industry building great mansions employ architects and construction workers, and buy lots of materials to build the monuments to their fortunes. They argue that the more wealth they acquire, the more they stimulate the economy, and thus everyone wins. My response: Is it better for our economy if one billionaire has five $10 million mansions . . . or if we build 250 $200,000 houses?

Most economists would argue it's the latter—but my aim with this example is not to advocate any particular economic theory. Instead, I am asking how the accumulation of more and more money benefits the individual. I am applying the same logic I've used throughout this chapter to my own situation: My life is more enjoyable without an addiction to wealth.

A good thing is just that: a good thing. Too much of a good thing is addiction.

CHAPTER 4

The Enemy Is Despair

I sincerely wish you will have the experience of thinking up a new idea, planning it, organizing it, and following it to completion and having it be magnificently successful. I also hope you'll go through the same process and have something "bomb out."

I wish you could know how it feels "to run" with all your heart and lose—horribly.

I wish that you could achieve some great good for mankind, but have nobody know about it except you.

I wish you could find something so worthwhile that you deem it worthy of investing your life.

I hope you become frustrated and challenged enough to begin to push back the very barriers of your own personal limitations.

I hope you make a stupid, unethical mistake and get caught red-handed and are big enough to say those magic words, "I was wrong."

I hope you give so much of yourself that some days you wonder if it is worth it all.

I wish for you a magnificent obsession that will give you a reason for living and purpose and direction in life.

I wish for you the worst kind of criticism for everything you do, because that makes you fight to achieve beyond what you normally would.

I wish for you the experience of leadership.

—Dr. Earl Reum

SO FAR WE'VE discussed anhedonia and addiction—and how the two feed off of one another. The third culprit in this trio of societal afflictions is despair.

Carol, a friend of mine who is a retired college dean, recently told me she is "learning now more than ever from those she teaches." In her retirement, she works among the poorest in the inner city of Columbus, Ohio.

It's interesting that this highly intelligent and educated woman feels she is learning from folks who are working toward their GEDs.

One of the things Carol is learning is that she can quickly identify who will ultimately get their GED and who will not.

She says it's as simple as noticing the ones who take credit for their failings in life as opposed to those who claim someone else caused their situation.

We meet victims every day. The people I work with are more varied than Carol's colleagues. Most are seeking to become entrepreneurs. Others are just friends or friends of friends who are making career or life changes. Many are from impoverished backgrounds. Others range from young people still in college, to the suddenly unemployed, to children of wealthy friends.

Carol taught me to create a filter. Filtering means that before jumping in to provide service for just anyone who asks, I must discern if my work has any potential outcome. Since time in this life is limited, it is important to quickly decipher who is serious about doing the work and who is not. It's easy for desperate people to say, "I'm willing." It's much harder to do the work it takes to follow through.

"My boss didn't appreciate my work." "My wife doesn't understand me." "I've never had a chance or I'd be a huge success." These are familiar refrains from prospective learners and entrepreneurs. Victims make poor learners because they ceaselessly identify problems they can't control rather than working on the only thing they can control: themselves.

In my first meeting with each person, I ask lots of questions about what they've experienced and what they hope to achieve.

Through this process, I can more easily identify victims and refer them elsewhere.

Victims and Learners

My friend Jim and I put one of his cooks in business about six years ago. She was a hard worker who seemed to never have a chance, so Jim decided to sell his seasonal restaurant to her. He came to me and said, "Help me get behind Jennifer. She's always wanted her own business, has a good family, and still remains one of the working poor." So, we got a bank to give her the loans she needed by guaranteeing their repayment.

We require all borrowers to meet with each other and us once a month, but Jennifer never made a meeting. After the first few meetings she missed, I visited to ask how she was. She said that she was just too busy.

"Okay," I said, "but you still need a business plan and measurements to check your progress, so let's just do those together."

"Great," she said . . . and then missed every project and deadline assigned to her.

Finally, in the third summer she owned the business, she revealed her real issue. She told me: "I know my business and you do not." She acknowledged that she was struggling, but said she knew what her problems were and she would fix them by herself if we would just leave her alone.

Having no other choice, we left her alone. Two years later,

the business went bankrupt amid a landslide of unpaid bills.

Her real problem was the same faced by others who decline any assistance because they "know" their problems. Victims follow the oft-cited definition of insanity: doing the same thing over and over and expecting different results. Those who overcome their problems usually do so by working on changing themselves and their approach to chronic problems. Victims tend to apply whatever solutions they know to problems beyond their control.

Victims rail against the storm that's sinking their boat and hold the tiller more tightly.

Learners step back and consider their options to change course. The best people to work with identify the nature of the storm but admit to their own mistakes. They ask for guidance in understanding how they got into the storm and what to learn from the situation.

In short, they see life's inequities as learning opportunities rather than as reasons to despair.

Those are the people I seek to work with because I've battled despair all my life.

We Have Met the Enemy and He Is . . .

Oliver Hazard Perry famously reported to General Benjamin Harrison during the War of 1812, "We met the enemy and they are ours."

Many years later, Pogo, Walt Kelly's comic strip character, said, "We have met the enemy and he is us."

My enemy was not my parents, though they were not perfect.

My enemy was not the guy who played defense across from me on the basketball court, and he most certainly was not the referee.

My enemy was not the other candidates for promotions in the advertising companies where I worked.

The enemies of my own businesses have never been my competition.

And my enemies were certainly not my brothers, sisters, wife, children, and other extended family members who have at times been difficult but have always been my teachers—both in good times and bad.

I've long since realized that despair is the only true enemy I've ever had.

Once convinced of this truth, I was able to free myself from working on things I cannot control. The focus was no longer about avoiding mistakes, but instead on shortening the recovery period between inevitably making mistakes and correcting them. We will all face failure—the question is whether or not we succumb to despair about our failures.

We began building our foundation in 1997. Its original function was direct service, but by the mid-2000s, we learned from our embarrassing mistakes and began focusing on "serving those who serve the poor" instead of working directly with the poor. In 2008, we reorganized under the name The Business of Good, and by late 2010 we had made a mess of things. In retrospect, the availability of so much money seemed to make us think too much of ourselves. We built a large board of directors and an office staff; making sizable donations to organizations we hardly knew anything about. In other words, we had become a traditional philanthropic organization.

It's embarrassing to look back on those early years of service. Since 2011, we've streamlined our organization and enjoyed relatively efficient outcomes, but we still make mistakes incessantly.

And so I've learned to begin each phase of planning by examining the work's current iteration. Each new plan starts with a detailed review of what seems to be working and what's not.

One of life's primary lessons for me is that the more willing I am to fail, the greater the potential of what we build. Great feats are never accomplished on the first attempt and rarely even on the second, third, or fourth attempt.

Great careers and great lives require constant adjustments. That's a lesson continually drilled into my consciousness whether building better businesses, charitable works, music performances, or really any other pursuit I've dedicated myself to over time.

You're Fired

This book began with the story of the one time I lost a full-time job. But I've been "fired" many times.

My first clear invitation to become a victim of my own despair happened when I was fired from a rock 'n' roll band. I was fifteen years old.

"Weed," the name of our band—which still prompts howls of laughter from my children—had grown from our garage to a fair level of success over the year I served as the lead singer. We put our hearts and souls into everything we did—getting gigs, practicing hard, getting out promotional material, and so on.

One day, after I had frozen onstage while singing a few days earlier and given a terrible performance, our lead guitarist heckled me at practice and we had a hell of a fight. The next day, the band's manager visited me and told me that the band members had voted me out of the group.

I was devastated. Not only because I'd lost my position in a dream project, but also by realizing my destruction was my own doing—first by my lousy performance, then by my stupid reaction.

I didn't eat much for two days and just moped around the house in my own personal pity party. My mom sensed that talking to me was hopeless, so at some point she decided just to make a decoupage of the Earl Reum poem that leads off this chapter. She left it on my bed one night. These few lines from her gift still stand out forty-five years later:

> *I hope you become frustrated and challenged enough to begin to push back the very barriers of your own personal limitations.*
>
> *I wish for you the worst kind of criticism for everything you do, because that makes you fight to achieve beyond what you normally would.*
>
> *I wish for you the experience of leadership.*

Since then, I've been fired twice more—once from a key account at an advertising agency and another time from my place of employment. In each case, I went back to Mom's poem, which I still keep at my desk, and try to remember that my only enemy is despair.

Seeing beyond Challenges

Another invitation to despair came in my forties when a good friend became the head of vocations for the Catholic Diocese of Cleveland. He asked me to be on his team to handle marketing. I blindly said, "Sure."

After some research about recruiting priests, I approached

Father Bob. "Let me get this straight," I said. "We have to convince young men that they should go to school for nine years after graduating high school."

"Right," he said.

"And they will be poor and lonely for those nine years, and when they graduate, they will take a vow of poverty for life."

"Yes, again."

"Okay, and they must also pledge a vow of obedience, which essentially means that whatever they are told to do by their superiors, they must do—whether they agree with it or not."

"Right."

"And they cannot date, get married, or engage in any form of sex."

"Yes."

"Oh, and even though 99 percent of all priests live entirely moral lives, many people will view these men as predators?"

"Indeed, Tim, many people now view me skeptically because of my collar."

"Bob, you need a different guy than me for this job."

"No I don't," he said, "because if you can't find the pony in this horse manure, I'm giving up too."

Given that Father Bob is the only person I know who is more tenacious than I am, I was swayed. I decided to take on the challenge. My first step was to interview current priests and seminarians to find out why they accepted such lousy conditions. After about thirty interviews, I understood more deeply than ever that despair can be avoided and life can be defined by service to others.

Here's what one elder priest told me, whose words reflect what most of the others had to say about their vocations: "I live a very full life," he said, "one I could not have lived in the secular world. I am connected to many people over their entire lives. To some I've been present at their birth, baptism, confirmation, marriage, and death. And I've been with their families throughout.

"When there is a need, a confidence, a mistake, or a great victory, they look to me as their soul mate. And the love and privilege that come from such a position are far more than I could have ever gained by worldly blessings."

I was deeply inspired.

In my twenties I began to keep a "pride" file. The idea came from a column I read in 1979 by advertising writer and columnist Whit Hobbs. In the file I place thank-you notes I've received or articles I've written that were published—anything I feel pride about. It's a great file to review when despair beckons.

If the elder priest I interviewed had a pride file, he would have needed a warehouse to store its contents. I have a file in a drawer. His life is certainly far more challenging than mine, and yet he is also better armed against the temptations of despair.

Everyone we know has challenges and those challenges either become their excuse for a sad life or barriers they surmount. It is no different for me. Despair, my enemy, visits often to invite me to give up again.

As of this writing, he's losing.

But I still have to get through today.

CHAPTER 5

Meet Mom and Dad

The world is too much with us; late and soon,
Getting and spending, we lay waste our powers;—
Little we see in Nature that is ours;
We have given our hearts away, a sordid boon!
This Sea that bares her bosom to the moon;
The winds that will be howling at all hours,
And are up-gathered now like sleeping flowers;
For this, for everything, we are out of tune;
It moves us not.

—William Wordsworth

LIKE ALL OF us, I'm the sum of all my experiences. And so, to tell my story, I have to go all the way to the beginning. It never surprises me when I look back and realize how great an impact my family had in forming my view of the world. And my family was both very different from and very similar to most American families in the 1950s and 1960s.

William and Margaret McCarthy raised ten children. Dad was a medical doctor, an abdominal surgeon, and Mom had been a journalist for the *Chicago Tribune* for ten years before marrying my dad after his first wife, Winifred Miller McCarthy, passed. My mom married my dad to raise his and Winnie's three young boys. Her doctor had told my mom that she would be unable to have children, so this seemed like a great option for a thirty-four-year-old career woman who had more or less given up on having her own family.

She then proceeded to have children in 1946, 1947, 1948, 1949, 1950, 1952 (me) and 1954.

I was the ninth of ten children. From my perch, the view of my family and our little world was interesting. My brothers Bill, Miller, and Terry were eleven, thirteen, and fourteen years older than me and became my early heroes; the five siblings closer to my age—Mary, Kathie, Steve, Sheila, and Felicia—grew up as my best friends; and my little sister, Janie, born with Down syndrome, taught me what little I know about true love and patience.

The most accurate description of the McCarthy home is something a New York City cabbie once said to me when I asked him to describe his city: "One word: more."

We had more tears and more laughs, more intelligence and more stupid human tricks, more fighting and more hugging, more bicycles and cars in the driveway, more friends and relatives in the house, more parties on more occasions, more bills to pay . . . and so forth.

There was always a lot going on.

There were a lot of lessons too, both good and bad. Mom and Dad's lesson of quiet service was among those that resonate to this day.

What I Learned from Jane Maura

My little sister Janie was born with Down syndrome.

I don't remember noticing it much as a young kid. She was just my little sister, and as such, she followed me around like any little kid would. I liked her and my friends did too, and so it just seemed natural to them and to me, although she certainly did look, walk, and talk quite differently from others.

One night, a couple was in the living room with my mother and they were crying. After she had seen them off, I asked my mom who they were.

"Lisa and Jim just found out their child has Down's, like Janie," she said. After some prompting, she then told me that the local association for mentally disabled citizens had been sending similar couples to her for years, usually at the time they were deciding whether to keep the child or have him or her institutionalized.

"Did you ever consider putting Janie in a home?" I asked.

"Why would we ever do that?" she responded.

From then on, I noticed when other Down parents called Mom, and one time I heard her say, "We are blessed to have Jane; she's a good teacher for our other kids."

That may seem counter-intuitive, but the stories of Jane's entertaining and teaching her brothers and sisters are endless. One of my favorites was when Jane grabbed my brother Steve's hand as he walked past her down the aisle at his wedding. When he leaned over, she cried, "I'm so happy!"

Another of our favorites unfolded when Jane first moved to my sister Mary's house when Mom and Dad were no longer able to care for her. Mary's husband Mel ran into Jane's new school principal at the grocery store after she had been at the school for about a week.

"Mel, we're glad to have Janie," the principal said, "and I'm so sorry about her speech problem."

"What speech problem?" Mel asked.

"Her not talking," the principal replied. "She hasn't spoken a word since she arrived, and we can't seem to get her to talk."

That night at dinner, Mel asked, "Jane, what's this about the school saying you don't talk?"

Jane looked down at her food and mumbled, "They pissed me off, Mel."

What I learned from Mom was that even in the most trying of circumstances (there are many difficult Jane stories also), gentle patience and unconditional love could make your own little world a brighter place.

What I learned from Jane was to live right smack dab inside the moment. As my son-in-law, Keith, says about his little brother, Jake, who also has Down syndrome: "He gets mad and gets over it."

Prescribing Fun

Recently, I ran into a nurse who was working as a clown at a local outdoor event. She told me she worked with my father for years and that it was he who inspired her to become a volunteer clown.

At home, Dad was mostly a stern presence to us, so I asked, "How did my dad make you want to be a clown?"

"He attended to his patients' minds and spirits," she said, "not just their bodies."

She told me about Dad whistling while he worked, even in the intensive care section of the hospital. She said it seemed he knew that if they all felt their doctor wasn't worried, they shouldn't worry.

One day, she was with him as he attended a dying patient, and he wrote a prescription for that patient and gave it to her to fill in the hospital pharmacy. After he left she read the prescription, which simply said, "M&Ms."

She ran down the hall after Dad, and when she caught up to him she said, "Doctor, do you mean candy?"

"Of course," he said. "It won't hurt her, and maybe it will give her a smile."

No Second Billing Notices

At Christmas time, I noticed that a lot of people stopped at our house with gifts. We knew many of them only as "Dad's patients."

One of our favorites was Joe Perry, the maintenance man at our school. Whenever Joe was at our house, he was fixing something, and whenever he was fixing something, he was talking. He was boisterous and always lovingly teasing us children. And mostly while teasing, he was also teaching.

One time, after Joe had shoveled our driveway, Dad offered him some money.

"No thanks, Doc. Merry Christmas."

This really hit me because I knew Joe worked three jobs to get by, including driving our school bus for extra cash. So I went straight to Joe the next time I saw him and asked him why he didn't take the money.

"Timmy," he said, "your dad has taken care of every one of my six kids, from bringing them into this world to every shot they needed or earache they needed fixed. And he's never sent me a bill. How much is that worth?"

My father's office nurse once told me that Dad's policy was to never send a second notice on a billing.

"If they haven't paid, they must not be able to afford it," he would tell her. And so he never achieved the big income most surgeons make.

Naive, yes—and the result was that we were never as rich as all the other doctors' families in town.

Back then I wondered why he couldn't have sent just a few of those notices so that I could have some extra things the other kids had. But now I know what he was teaching us.

We didn't travel the world or belong to country clubs like our neighbors and cousins, but we lived in a lovely home on a beautiful street right on Lake Erie. Our neighborhood was real-life *Leave It to Beaver*: nice neighbors, a dad always in a suit, a mom who stayed home and kissed him on arrival and departure, five bedrooms, a couple nice cars in the garage, and lots of food on our table.

The local country club was five hundred yards from our house, and yet we never belonged to it. We only caddied there in the summer and rode sleds on its hills in the winter. A lovely boat club was similarly close, and yet Dad never belonged there either; in fact he never owned a boat. If asked, he would only say that he preferred spending his money and his time with his family in the home he referred to as "his castle."

The Perfect Parents

Of course we all know the perfect parents don't exist, and Mom and Dad were no exception, any more than Alice and I are to our children or they will be to theirs.

My mom was a great procrastinator. She often told me that cleaning her house was wearing her out. But actually, our house was so dirty that it was clear to me that it was the *worrying* about cleaning her house that "wore her out."

Mom was also legendarily passive-aggressive. Sweetly, she would manipulate all of us to go exactly where she wanted us. Guilt was not a weapon for my mom; it was an IED (improvised explosive device).

My dad had no moral flexibility. None. There was a right and there was a wrong, and even hearing there might be a gray area between black and white would send him into frenzy. He also had no patience with adolescent behavior and would likely today be diagnosed with OCD. One example of this is that he probably never went more than an hour without washing his hands at our kitchen sink—with prescription-strength antibacterial soap!

Dad's IED was intimidation; he had a glare that would melt metal and a very sharp tongue. When my siblings or I were acting up, he could silence us with one look or by clearing his throat. We knew better than to make him mad enough to talk!

Mom's Final Interview

In 1998, years after Dad was gone and only a year before Mom passed, my sister Kathie and I did a long interview with Mom. One of the questions was, "Did Dad ever regret not being wealthy like Uncle John, who was also an MD?"

"If he was alive," she said, "he'd tell you that he was very wealthy, and not just because of you kids. He grew up in a three-bedroom house in downtown Findlay with five siblings, and yet he raised you all in a beautiful five-bedroom house on the shores of Lake Erie. His dad scraped by selling insurance and still got all his kids through college, and yet your dad had a great home, a new car every two years, and he spent all of his time and money on us. No, Tim, he respected his wealthy brother, John, but he felt he was as rich as he wanted to be."

As an adult, I came to realize that Dad valued money, but just enough that he could live the way he wanted to without becoming so wealthy he might get lost in it.

I strive for a similar balance. The learning that came from having such educated and accomplished professionals as parents who found better use for their skills than material wealth came to me later, but very powerfully.

Due to what could be called Dad's poor business skills or his great compassion, Mom shopped at the Goodwill Thrift Store, turned the thermostat down to sixty every night, and shared everything she had, most of all her good nature and incredible listening skills. As her children left the nest, she made Sunday nights her time at her old typewriter, writing each of us a letter with the news in our town or about each other. If those envelopes had contained a thousand dollars, they wouldn't have been received more gratefully than they were with nothing more than her messages of interest and love.

And while Mom didn't volunteer formally (what mother of ten has time?), her availability to anyone who needed her was legendary. I remember her leaving family parties to answer calls from friends who needed her "right then." She hated flying, and yet she took airplanes to see her siblings and to be with her ten children soon after they delivered each of her twenty-eight grandchildren.

Sure, You Can Have a Bike

The most enduring gift Mom and Dad gave all ten of us was their abiding faith that hard work and education create independence.

When I was nine, I asked Dad for a bike because several kids in the neighborhood had gotten one for Christmas. "Sure, you can have one," Dad said. "Take some of your brother's paper route, and you'll save up enough in no time."

I remember hating the job because I had to get up so early to deliver the morning paper, and then still catch the bus to school. Worst of all were the Saturdays when I had to go "collecting." I hated asking for money!

But every Saturday, I delivered all I collected (except for one dollar for baseball cards) to my mom, and one year later, she told me I had enough to buy the Schwinn Spitfire I'd been eyeing all along. Today I can still see my hands putting down $53.28 on Mr. Baker's counter. I can remember riding it, washing it, and putting baseball cards in the spokes to create sound, all the while knowing this bike was not a gift—it was mine. Mom and Dad couldn't tell me what to do with my bike because I bought it.

Alice and I provided more materially to our three children than my parents did to us, but the one lesson we remembered was to insist that they work once they reached their teens, which all three did.

My brothers and I disagreed strongly over this point.

"What is a kid going to learn after their first week at McDonald's?" my brother once asked me.

"Life," was my answer, and that would have been my mom and dad's answer too.

Working teens learn early that work can be fun on some nights and horrible on others; that your supervisors have power that is often wielded unkindly; and that Uncle Sam takes a lot out of your paycheck. They also learn that some days you watch the clock and other days you leave work exhausted, and that some of your best friends are found through mutual suffering and success in the workplace.

Many parents do not allow their children to work and then later wonder why those same kids cannot balance life and work as adults. That uncertainty shows a lack of faith in our kids. One friend actually told me, "I must include my kids in my wealth planning because they will not have the same opportunities I had—no matter how smart and hard-working they are."

Really? Do we really think smart, hard-working people will go out of style?

This need to help our children avoid some dreaded future is best expressed by a reader of mine whose definition of "adequate wealth" included "providing for family members I will never know."

It would exhaust me (and frankly embarrass my children) if I thought so little of them that I felt I had to provide for them and their children's children.

Only now, did the point of Mom and Dad's approach come to fruition. That is, once you've gained the comfortable lifestyle that America uniquely offers, piling up more money is like spilling gasoline onto the pavement after your tank is full: meaningless, empty abundance.

Wealth Is a Burden?

Mom gave me her last lesson about money a few months before she passed in 1999.

I wanted her to know before she passed that my company looked like it would succeed and that as a result, I would become a very wealthy man.

When I told her this, she said, "Oh, honey, I'm so sorry."

I could only look at her stunned and say, "What?"

"Wealth is a burden, Timmy," she replied. "And I worry how you will carry it."

I was aghast, reminding her that I'd been mostly a good guy, faithful to my family, a churchgoer—and that I also served the poor!

And she just smiled lovingly and said, "Honey, I've seen better people than you changed by money."

Wow, that one hurt! But the result of her jarring comment was that I am ever vigilant to the cause of remaining myself in all my goodness and badness. I must also pay the thought forward to my children by example, by simply being who I am.

• • •

My daughter, Caitlin, occasionally sends me collections of songs she enjoys and learns from. I remember a song on one of her collections sent in 2003 by Jack Johnson titled "Gone":

Cars and phones and diamond rings,
Bling, bling, because those are only removable things.
And what about your mind? Does it shine?
Are there things that concern you, more than your time?

Mom and Dad felt the same way I do. I will be ever less concerned with my children's wealth than I am with their independence. Or, as Mr. Johnson put it, do their minds shine?

CHAPTER 6
_____

Creating Success

Advertising is a simple business made difficult by complicated people.
—Draper Daniels

CREATING BUSINESS AND financial success was extremely difficult for me—but it was never complicated.

Simplicity beats complexity every day of the week, and further, kindness and fairness outweigh obsession and drive. Contrary to many hard-edged theories of business building, treating others as you wish to be treated is an effective approach to winning at business.

How quaint.

You Can't Teach an Empty Bag to Stand Up Straight

When I was starting my business, I read a small Ken Blanchard and Norman Vincent Peale book titled *The Power of Ethical Management*. The most memorable lesson from the book is to treat each associate as if they are a bank account; that is, to consider each interaction with another person as either a deposit or a withdrawal.

Commend them for doing something right, you're making a deposit in their self-esteem bank. Deal with them respectfully even while correcting a mistake, another deposit. Listen patiently when something is bothering them, another deposit. Conversely, of course, you're making a withdrawal if you dress them down in front of others, are too busy to listen to their concerns, and forget to praise.

And as in our bank accounts, if we make more deposits than withdrawals, there are "savings" to draw from. So, when I make a hurtful mistake or need extra effort or time from an associate, there is something in their "self-esteem bank" for me to withdraw. But if we continually make more withdrawals than deposits, there is nothing in reserve when we need forgiveness or extra effort.

Sounds obvious, huh? So why do so many employers make so many withdrawals from the bank of our spirits?

Profitable Kindness

The Blanchard–Peale theory is abstract, so let's go to the restaurant business for a concrete example.

For over thirty years I've been associated with restaurant chains, and many of them use the following line of thinking: "Pay people poorly and push them hard, and you will make a profit. This is a tough business so you must run over people or get run over yourself."

Don't believe this? Visit any restaurant in your town and observe how supervisors talk with employees. We are typically a cold-hearted business, smiling at our customers while kicking our employees in the butt.

It never made any sense to me. Who thinks that after you yell at an employee they are likely to go out and be nice to a customer?

To suggest that success is created through kindness may seem soft, so here is a specific, current example.

My son Tim owns a restaurant chain, Raising Cane's of Ohio, that as of this writing has over six hundred employees, about 540 of whom live on the margins of society. They are hourly restaurant workers living mostly from paycheck to paycheck.

Despite earning millions in revenues, Tim claims he owns

a "social business." That is, he believes that Cane's secret to financial success is that they provide a safe and fun place for their hourly employees to spend a significant portion of their lives each week.

Here are some of the innovative approaches that he has applied in his business over the last ten years:

> Paying well over the minimum wage.

> Sharing profits with all, even temporary, employees.

> Following a zero-tolerance policy regarding verbal abuse. (I've seen them fire a great general manager because he yelled at a worker!)

> Sharing with every Cane's worker every financial fact about the business and holding regular meetings where they can learn what the numbers mean.

> Depositing fifty dollars monthly into a prepaid debit card for every employee to use on any health care need.

> Recognizing employees on a monthly, quarterly, and annual basis—unfailingly. One of my favorites happens in May when, on Mother's Day, all employees are invited to bring their moms or "anyone who acts like their mother" in for two free meals.

And here's the punch line: Tim's reward for being "nice" is that he operates one of the most profitable chains in the country, one that will be very valuable only a few years from now.

Measuring the Golden Ruler

Having bought into the Blanchard–Peale theory, I decided that the only mission statement my first business would have was the Golden Rule: "Treat others as you wish to be treated."

We chose to avoid long-winded and unattainable mission statements about putting our people, stakeholders, and customers first. Instead, we chose the above eight words that truly tested our commitment to our employees, customers, and vendors. The statement is so strong that it is hard to hide behind. The danger of making such a statement is you must be able to teach and live it.

Training to such a simple, compelling mission statement was tricky at first. We posed various difficult, hypothetical situations involving customers, fellow workers, bosses, and vendors to our employees. After each case in point, we'd ask them to come up with a solution using "treat others as you wish to be treated." Let's say it was a vendor who had screwed up. Should you yell at the vendor, fire them, or ask them what they'd be willing to do to make things right?

It is a difficult mission to uphold. The toughest case for me happened with a huge client who was chronically abusive to our employees. . . .

The Day I Fired Back

Twice I'd heard stories of our database person being brought to tears by a client's creative director. After the second incident, I called our client's senior vice president of marketing and told him of the specific situations. He said kindly, "I'm not sure at all about your accusation but I will check it out, and I can assure you we do not tolerate such behavior."

"That's good," I said, relieved, "because if it does happen again, we would have to resign your account."

He was pretty surprised by that statement, but I had said it firmly but kindly, so he responded, "Okay, I understand your position."

A couple weeks went by and sadly, it happened again. I called my client and asked to see him in person. He accepted, and I remember to this day how anxious I was as I travelled to his office. These guys represented over 10 percent of our business, and the reason I am not mentioning any names here is that they are a globally respected brand.

When I delivered the news to Jim that we were resigning his account because the verbal abuse had happened again, he said, "Tim, I'll try again to get this to stop, but you can't just walk away."

"I can and I am," I said. "But we'll give you ninety days and provide a smooth transition once you find a suitable vendor. I told you a couple weeks ago that we have to make good on our mission statement or it's useless."

I never talked about this action with anyone except for our CEO, but there was a buzz at the office for the rest of that week. And to this day, part of the company's folklore is "the day we fired the big client."

Unemotional Numbers

My favorite advertising mentor was Jim Johnson. He had a brilliant mind plus credentials from Tuck School of Business at Dartmouth. As executive vice president of McCann–Erickson, the United States' largest advertising agency, his smarts were legendary.

One day, in the middle of a huge campaign development project for a very large client, Jim called me out on "creating numbers." What he meant was that my report cited perhaps twenty-five different entries when maybe a half dozen would have been sufficient for the analysis I was doing for the client.

"We create advertising, McCarthy. Keep it simple and let the numbers speak for themselves."

Jim lectured the assembled team, telling them that great business and financial plans do not require algebra or trigonometry. They require attention to simple mathematics. "All you need to create a business plan is a pencil and a calculator. Our calculations must be tight—but no more complex than addition, subtraction, multiplication, and division. The numbers may be huge, but the disciplines for driving profit are not complicated and they do not change."

Unemotional Language

Jim also taught us that better business writing is equally simple.

Every new account manager received a book from Jim titled *The Elements of Style*. This classic text provides the principal requirements of plain English style. It names the rules of usage and principles of composition—most of which are still commonly violated almost one hundred years after the first edition of the manuscript was written.

One day I dropped off a business plan for a key client in Jim's office. Less than an hour later, Jim was in my office saying, "Nouns and verbs, Tim. Nouns and verbs."

"What does that mean?" I asked.

"I'm not paying you to be a poet or novelist," Jim responded. "So we can get rid of all the adjectives, adverbs, metaphors, and so forth. Tell them what they need to know. That is all."

As businesses get larger, we are tempted to believe more complicated formulas for success are needed. They are not. A famous Steve Jobs sentiment (perhaps borrowed from Einstein) is that nature craves simplicity. And his was a rather large, complicated business named Apple.

Larger problems are naturally complex, but their solutions need not be.

Business to Business . . . to Consumer

Our first company, WorkPlace Media, was based on a unique and simple idea: deliver coupons to where people work versus where they live. Since print media coupons are a $5 billion category, we were able to create a solid middle-market niche company. The concept was simple and scalable. Ultimately we made friends at over seven hundred thousand private employers in the United States with between fifty and five hundred employees. Using our service, huge clients such as McDonald's, LensCrafters, and Goodyear were able to send incentives to as few as five thousand people near one store or to as many as seventy million with a national coupon drop. Yet each coupon was custom-packaged and delivered to a person—our key contact—at each target employer.

Building such a system was certainly complicated, but the concept never changed. We were making friends at employers who would then share our samples with their associates. This was a classic "win–win": The employer got a free benefit, the advertiser got noticed in an uncluttered environment, and we got paid for making that connection effectively.

Ordinary People; Extraordinary Achievement

But the success story of WorkPlace goes beyond the initial concept. It was more about the people involved. And luckily, we were able to retain our best people. The atmosphere we fostered at WorkPlace created stability: our top five officers were with us an average of thirteen years out of the nineteen we owned the business.

Our CEO, Pat White, had taken a twenty-five-year break from teaching to raise her children. Eight years after re-entering the workforce as a phone operator for us, she took over the company.

Several senior managers, whom we found in unusual places, aided Pat. Our COO was a junior-level operations manager at a local manufacturer; our CTO was recruited from her parents' video store, where she was languishing after getting her computer science degree; and our best salesman came to us not long after failing in his own business venture.

The tracks of these extraordinary lives are another focal point for creating success. None of these people were ideally trained to run a highly profitable and successful business. And yet they were able to do just that for two key reasons: They all had an insatiable appetite for learning and they each represented the very soul of perseverance.

The best people (as well as the best organizations) I've known are the ones who are "works in progress." They try to be aware of their weaknesses and strengths and deal with both directly. We often said, "We are twice as good as we were last year and only half as good as we will be next year."

Success or Meaning?

Obviously I'm proud of WorkPlace Media, but I also feared its success would define me, as often happens with start-up entrepreneurs. This was something I actively tried to avoid. If I couldn't avoid it . . . who would I be after the business was no longer mine?

I had a cousin who was a Catholic priest, and I went to the fiftieth anniversary of his ordination. There were two cardinals in attendance—that's how well respected my cousin was, although he remained a parish priest throughout his life. The church was packed with people who came to hear my cousin give the homily, and I was really looking forward to it. I was a young man at the time, in my twenties, and I was ready to hear some really good tips on living.

But when my cousin stood up, before the cardinals and dozens of other priests and hundreds of members of his Cleveland parish, he never once mentioned himself. He never once mentioned all the respected, accomplished churchmen behind the altar with him. He did not detail his career as I expected, nay, hoped that he would. Instead, he talked about his passion: young people. He pleaded with us to recommit our lives to encouraging young people we knew with our love and example. He was a man who lived a full life, not because of his place or position, but because he put his heart and soul into helping others fulfill *their* vocations. To me, that's a life of significance.

Following the precepts outlined in this chapter brought me success in business. But even now, a bigger challenge remains, which is the central question of my search: How do I continually apply the rules for creating a successful business venture to creating a significant, more satisfying life?

CHAPTER 7

Finding Significance

*The more one forgets himself—by giving himself to
a cause to serve or another person to love—the more
human he is and the more he actualizes himself. What
is called self-actualization is not an attainable aim
at all, for the simple reason that the more one would
strive for it, the more he would miss it. In other words,
self-actualization is possible only as a side-effect of self-
transcendence.*

—Viktor Frankl

I WAS ONLY twenty-five when I first read Frankl's *Man's Search for
Meaning,* and while I wasn't mature enough to entirely understand its precepts, the book pointed me in the right direction.

Frankl was a psychiatrist who lived in Nazi concentra-
tion camps from 1944 to 1945, and lost his wife, mother, and

brother in the Holocaust. His primary discovery from those horrible years was the importance of finding meaning in all forms of existence, even the most sordid ones, and thus a reason to continue living.

"I saw the truth as it is set into song by so many poets," says Frankl, "proclaimed as the final wisdom by so many thinkers. The truth: that love is the ultimate and the highest goal to which man can aspire."

Frankl's thinking came back to me recently when an associate told me, "The biggest problem for me is that too often I don't know what I want, so I wind up chasing things that don't matter."

I'd witnessed Mom and Dad finding their significance, but Dr. Frankl's work convinced me that I could overcome my melancholy and live a fuller life in love. And since service—which is really just another word for love—became the focus of my life, my life matters more than it ever did before.

Wealth by itself is unsatisfying. This is a lesson learned from experience. Providing service to others has been what has brought meaningful, lasting satisfaction to my life: It has been my antidote to anhedonia. But discovering this truth was no easy path—and even after I had discovered it, I continued to falter in executing it, even still to this day. I learned in my stumbling that unstructured, unaccountable charity helps neither the giver nor the receiver. *Mindful giving*, on the other hand, brings me deep life satisfaction—and creates sustainable, meaningful change in the world.

In the early chapters of this book, we looked at the problems of anhedonia, addiction, and despair in American society. I've told the stories of how these afflictions have affected my life—and the journey I've taken both in my personal life and in my business life to overcome them. In this and the following chapters of the book, I'll share how I finally began to solidify my approach to living meaningfully, with the key being mindful giving. I'll explain what the word "mindful" means to me, and I'll discuss the strategies I've developed for giving time and treasure.

Mindful giving might not prove to be your truth, but these lessons are a template for finding whatever does prove to be your truth. And if it happens to include mindful giving, you'll learn some clues for how to go about it!

Fairly Lenient

My first job after college was as the executive director of the Republican Committee of Oakland County, Michigan. It was there that I worked for my first great mentor, Arthur G. Elliott.

Art was successful by most measures. His construction company made him a wealthy man. His status as the right-hand man to then-governor and presidential candidate George

Romney made him relatively famous. And his wife and three sons adored him.

While confident publicly, Art was a humble man who every morning could be found saying his daily lessons in the quiet of the hallway near his bedroom.

I learned an extraordinary number of practical lessons from Art. He was a hard-edged businessman who could forecast and balance his books to the penny while simultaneously concentrating on building up the people around him.

A few months into my tenure as his director, Art sat me down and let me know that I would be moving on to a new career if I didn't "straighten up and fly right." Over the course of a long discussion, Art made it clear to me that it wasn't enough for all the volunteers and donors to love me. He said in very strong terms that I was not there to be elected. I was there to plan, organize, and control a party organization.

A few days after chewing me out, he asked me why I seemed down, and I responded that no one had ever spoken to me so harshly. I will never forget his response that day in 1976. He said, "Our society wants to replace the concept of fairness with leniency, Tim. I will not be lenient with you because you have great potential. You must be fair with me, and I must strive to be fair rather than lenient with you. When you mess up, you deserve to know it and to know why. When you do well, rest assured I will reward you materially as well as with my moral support."

It was a lesson every altruistic person should learn, and it was a turning point for my bleeding heart. I've learned since then to be fair rather than lenient, and that has helped greatly in my own search for significance.

All Used Up When We Die

There's an old story about football-coaching great Vince Lombardi standing in front of his team after a tough loss with a football in his hand saying, "Tomorrow, we are going back to the fundamentals. We will start by teaching you that this"—he pointed to the ball—"is a football."

It is said that a grizzled old veteran, Fuzzy Thurston, responded by saying, "Wait a minute, Coach, you're going too fast for me."

The "football" in my life is my search for meaning. That has never changed—it is my spiritual center. Fundamental meaning can only be found within. Early in my life I became a searcher.

A friend recently wrote me: "I still feel that I have not been successful in life, and therefore find myself sometimes feeling stuck between being happy with my life and being disappointed. I just have such a great feeling deep inside my soul that there is another purpose for my life and that much greater happiness and successes await me, which makes me always try to progress toward something greater than what I have today."

My own search for meaning has taken me both on a journey into my Catholic faith and—with similar vigor—on a trip to Pleasure Island. (On the latter voyage, I was fortunate that Jiminy Cricket stayed with me, though I do remember trying to strangle him a few times.) The search has also taken me to life-altering books such as Frankl's and another wonderful book by Harold Kushner titled *When All You've Ever Wanted Isn't Enough*. And the search led me into a mindfulness meditation practice at forty-five and to graduate school at fifty-three.

I've built my brain and heart through seemingly endless education on seemingly endless topics from business to religion to philanthropy to self-help.

Today, the search *is* the destination, and it will never end. Like George Bernard Shaw wrote in the preface to *Man and Superman*, "I want to be thoroughly used up when I die." Turning my life's "brief candle" into a "splendid torch" (words Shaw borrowed from Shakespeare) is, for me, the very spice of life.

Unapologetically Jake

As you find yourself, finding your significance becomes easier. And my significance is not yours or anyone else's.

Age has something to do with it and nothing to do with it. But don't take my word for it—take it from some of my closest friends and readers.

"I'm feeling better in my fifty-year skin than I ever felt in my twenties, thirties, and forties," says my friend Dave. "Peace/acceptance/patience definitely come with age! I am generally happy with my life, although I do wish I could go back in time and shake my younger self and say, 'Slow down—pay attention to the moment you have right now.' In hindsight, I was also way too concerned with what others thought about me—part of embracing fifty to me is finally having the courage to speak up about my beliefs and not compromise to keep the peace or the status quo."

On the other hand, my friend Jake, who died at age thirty-six, managed to find significance while he held his brief torch, even without the benefit of age's perspective. One day, long before he was ill, I apologized for being hard on him. Jake told me, "Tim, be unapologetically you because there is no one else who can do it for you. And I can learn more from who you are than I can from who I want you to be."

Jake's years on this Earth were abundant. He built a business, a family, and a wide circle of friends and admirers in a town that appeared to have been forgotten.

And his legacy to me includes learning that our own significance—in whatever pursuit we choose—is enough.

To Boldly Go Where I'd Never Gone Before

As my business began to profit in 1997, I formed Free Hand, Inc., a foundation named after my mother's plea: "If you don't give with a free hand, don't bother giving."

We funded the foundation with 25 percent of our company's net profit, which at first meant a few thousand dollars annually, but by 2003 was well over $250,000 each year.

Especially after bootstrapping and building a highly successful business, you would think building a service organization would be relatively easy. Yet the early years of learning my role in service, and therefore my own significance, were rocky.

My inspiration for service at that time was a Catholic priest named Norm Smith who took me to the St. Clair–Superior neighborhood in Cleveland and asked me to help him partner with the poorest of our city's poor. A group of us from Norm's suburban parish then spent the next ten years developing nine services for the neighborhood's poor based in the physical plant of the St. Philip Neri Parish at E. Eighty-Second Street and St. Clair Boulevard.

We converted the abandoned convent to three apartments to temporarily house refugees from war-torn regions such as Bosnia and the Sudan. We supported the development of a wonderful health ministry called "Project Hope" based in the abandoned school's cafeteria. We bought a van and transported folks to the soup kitchen on Wednesdays and every other Sunday. We eventually created a jobs reference center and a home health care and janitorial school. And the nuns from a nearby order came three days a week to tutor young and old who wanted to learn. We even handled the music ministry on Sundays for the forty or fifty neighborhood folks who showed up for ten o'clock mass . . . usually twenty or thirty minutes late.

Each time I experienced a deep feeling of service during these ten years, I was reminded to keep the "business of business" in perspective. The worst experiences I had—an exhausting week of travel or a particularly stinging client defeat—would often be followed by a meaningful experience in service to others.

It's Their Only Way Out

For me, inspiration often comes from watching those who work with the poor directly. On the St. Philip Neri campus, Rose Marie headed the health project with her husband, Noel. Theirs was a true Robin Hood story: Most of the things she provided the poor were "robbed" from the rich. Rose had a nursing degree and lots of contacts in the medical field, and most days I'd see or hear her coaxing someone to give their leftover time and materials.

A podiatrist came in to perform check-ups on Friday afternoons. A nutritionist spoke while folks were eating their free lunches. (They had to listen.) Dental students checked teeth, pharmacists brought information and samples of preventative products, nurses checked blood pressure—the list goes on and on.

Once or twice a month after a meeting, I would stick around to observe the beehive of activity that had become our service center.

One day, I watched nuns tutor school-aged kids and help older folks study for the GED. One young student was really giving an elderly nun a hard time. But she persisted until he settled down and eventually took his assignment, and she moved on to the next table.

After class, I asked that particular nun why she persisted with this service when she had obviously retired long ago. She simply answered, and I'll never forget, "It's their only way out."

Right now, writing these words, I'm clouding up—as I did that day. What she said was so poignant. If the poor, particularly the generational poor, cannot be educated, they quite literally (with the very occasional exception of professional athletes) cannot break the cycle of poverty.

As I gathered myself, I said to Sister Ann, "But isn't it time for you to rest? You've been teaching all your life."

"Without the work in hope of change," she said, "my life would have no meaning." She was succeeding, in other words, in her search for meaning.

One day I asked Father Norm, our leader in these works, "Why do we have so much fun doing what appears to be a very difficult job?"

He responded, "Because we get way more out of this than they do!"

Significant Humor

There are dozens of Father Norm stories, but my favorite will always be when he taught me to fight fire with humor.

One night we were headed to a meeting in which we knew our partner parishioners were going to express their anger about the work we were doing for refugees. They felt we should instead be solely focused on their neighbors. Norm asked me to pick him up on my way downtown, and when Norm answered the door at the parish, he was in a full clown costume. The whole nine yards: painted face, nose, and big floppy shoes—the works.

"Norm, get dressed," I said, "we're gonna be late for the meeting."

He instead closed the door behind him and headed for the car.

"Norm, what the hell are you doing? Why are you dressed like that?"

"Tim," he said, "it could get tough down there tonight. I gotta be ready for them."

Sure enough, the tension in the room dissipated the moment

Father walked in. In fact, the place broke up in laughter. People couldn't stop laughing even as they were complaining.

Norm passed suddenly in 2004. I never wondered if he had found his significance.

And since I'm an anxious person myself, as are many who choose service, the memories of Norm's significant humor comes in very handy while building our foundation.

The Soul of Collaboration

Since those days, we've transformed the foundation using the same iterative process I used to build my business.

In 2007, Catholic Charities took over our work at St. Philip Neri, and while the specific story of that transition is not pleasant, it drove us to become a more productive foundation. In short, the larger organization dispatched us from our work, saying we were no longer needed. And, once again, learning from our failure seemed to be a precursor to our success.

In 2008, we renamed the organization The Business of Good and firmly recommitted to the concept that we do not serve the poor but instead serve those who serve the poor. The poor remain our sole focus, but we reach them differently, and we think more effectively than we did in those days at St. Philip Neri.

We remain a private operating non-profit, a 501(c)(3), but we now center all of our work on fifteen non-profit partners whose efforts to serve the poor are aided by our business-forged discipline. Said differently, they do the service work, while we teach them to create and execute better business plans.

After seven years of planning, testing, and adjusting, we now realize we work better virtually. We have a managing director who is a contract employee, and each of our primary efforts (currently micro-lending, supporting first-generation college students, and creating a payday lending alternative) is accomplished entirely by the partners we serve with our time and money. We have no official office and no employees. We also measure our impact by how many other foundations we can bring to the table to collaborate on specific projects rather than just ourselves.

The summarizing lesson of these experiences is that significance is found in collaboration. The world of non-profits does not need more organizations; it needs more effective partnering among existing organizations dedicated to similar causes.

Spalding, You'll Get Nothing, and Like It!

Should my significance be the same as my children's and their children's?

The history of generational wealth says yes. My path goes in a different direction.

Warren Buffett once said, "I want to give my kids just

enough so that they would feel like they can do anything, but not so much that they would feel like doing nothing."

The first draft of our last will and testament included a letter to our children, which stated that by the time they were grown, we would have already given them the most valuable things anyone can ever receive: (1) unconditional love, (2) a good example, and (3) a good education.

At the end of our letter, we remind them that we are confident that they will use this inheritance wisely and pass on those specific gifts. These sentiments have not changed.

Today, the will reads that one percent of our estate's value will go to each of our three children. It seems a nice goodbye, and yet it is not sufficient to spoil them in any way.

The other 97 percent will remain in The Business of Good Foundation, which we hope they (and their children and cousins) will take control of someday. By the time they do, there will be no instructions left on how to sustain and grow the current mission. I refuse to try to "rule from the grave" as so many of my friends seem to think they can do. In fact, there will not even be strictures on the mission itself, other than to continue to find ways to make the world a better place. It will be up to them to interpret new meaning for that mission as their world changes.

What If None of This Works?

My favorite contemplative writer, Thomas Merton, said:

> *Do not depend on the hope of results. . . . [Y]ou may have to face the fact that your work will be apparently worthless and even achieve no result at all, if not perhaps results opposite to what you expect. As you get used to this idea, you start more and more to concentrate not on the results, but on the value, the rightness, the truth of the work itself. . . . [G]radually you struggle less and less for an idea and more and more for specific people. . . . In the end, it is the reality of personal relationships that saves everything.*

In my own journey toward significance, I remind myself of Merton's words often. And I've learned, the joys are in the moments of truth: firing a client who mistreated an associate or picking up Father Norm in his clown costume.

For whatever path to gaining significance you choose, and whether you can commit five hours, five dollars, or five million dollars to the task, there is no far-off destination. In fact there are only some moments you feel better about yourself while you're trying to make someone else feel better about themselves.

My peaceful nature—my good angel—accepts that I can only do so much and that the most important accomplishments will be in this moment. Am I treating the person I'm with in a manner that adds to their dignity? Those are the moments we actually do the most in "making the world a better place."

My ambitious nature—which also serves as my bad angel—directs me to find a greater role for business in meeting the needs of our broken world. The task I have in mind is so overwhelming that it is hard to describe.

But innovation is an iterative process, and Merton and Norm beckon me to take myself less seriously. So I rest in the knowledge that things may get better just by my trying. And I will also define my own significance by doing so.

CHAPTER 8

Heroes Still Walk This Earth

MOTHER TERESA, MAHATMA Gandhi, Nelson Mandela, and the Dalai Lama are heroes most of us are aware of, and all deserve to be emulated. But they are distant to me. And what they did seems unattainable.

So the heroes I emulate tend to be more down-to-earth. All are wounded to a certain extent. These heroes walk in our midst every day. In fact, all of us are heroes in the moments we genuinely reach outside of ourselves. And we need heroes in our lives. The path toward significance and meaning isn't easy. We need to be able to look to the people who have walked ahead of us—the people who have walked well—for encouragement and sometimes for the helpful reminder that it's okay to stumble. In this chapter, I will tell you about the heroes—large and small—who've informed my journey toward a life of mindful giving.

Most of my heroes are volunteers, and they show up everywhere, every day. They can be seen at the local library, museum, hospital, park, church, hospice, legal clinic, food bank, and other well-known public places. You will find them easily the next time you look.

These folks take no pay because they want to help and experience the joy of sharing. And they often change someone's life in very fundamental ways. As importantly, they change their own lives. A friend's wife passed many years ago, and he was so appreciative of her hospice care that he volunteered with that hospice organization for many years. Eventually they asked Jerry to take a fulltime job as a caregiver. His wife's legacy now includes the many lives he's affected since she passed.

Because of our work, I witness heroes with more far-reaching impact as well.

How Could You Be Smiling at a Time Like This?

Joe Cistone and I became friends when he volunteered at St. Philip Neri while we were developing the service center. In 2001, Joe became CEO of International Partners in Mission. IPM serves the poorest of the poor by supporting community-based projects in Central America, South Asia, and sub-Saharan Africa.

The original work we did with IPM included such simple gestures as sending our bookkeeper to their office on Friday afternoons to try to piece together their finances. Prior to Joe's arrival, IPM had been the classic "God will take care of things" organization. They held substantial debt and barely enough income to serve their partners and keep the lights on. Within four years, Joe had eliminated their debt and grown their income four-fold.

One of the primary ways we grew their mission was by creating "immersion experiences." People interested in seeing IPM-supported projects firsthand paid for the privilege of doing so—often in groups—and IPM made money from the trips. Over time, Alice, the kids, and I went on three trips with IPM.

On our first trip, Alice and I found ourselves in the bed of a pickup truck on the seventh day of an eight-day trip to El Salvador with Joe. We were headed back to a slum known as El Zeita, near San Salvador. There, we would meet with women who were trying to sell handmade clothing to support a school for their kids.

I was tired, hungry, and sweaty. I'd slept little since we'd been there as the accommodations were Spartan and—to be kind—it's a grim place. The night before, we were stopped by the local police, and Joe had walked around to the back of the van to talk with them. As he had suspected, they told him he could avoid court if he paid his fine right there by giving them everything he had in his wallet. When he climbed back in the van, he told us not to worry because shakedowns were normal, so he'd put just enough in his wallet to please them, while his "real" cash was in his sock.

On that seventh day, we passed another pickup truck, in the bed of which were six teenagers armed to the teeth. El Salvador has a long history of violence, and paramilitary "soldiers" were everywhere. I first saw them at the doors of the convenience stores we entered for supplies as we left on our daily trips.

As I was spitting out the dust from the pickup with the teen soldiers in it, I turned to see Joe leaning up against the back of the cab, his arms crossed and a peaceful smile across his face.

"Joe," I asked, "what the hell are you smiling about?"

"It's funny you ask. I was just thinking that this is where I belong. If I didn't have my daughter and my responsibilities back home, I'd move here."

I was aghast. All I could say was, "Joe, I will never understand you." Shortly after, with him still smiling at me, I asked, "What time does our damn plane get us out of here tomorrow?"

Joe is a hero walking in our midst. He is someone who would gladly give up America's materially abundant lifestyle for a life spent entirely among the very poor. And Joe is also a regular guy with lots of issues. In other words, he's just like us.

Leaving the Mansion in the Middle of the Night

Brad Roller has been a close friend for almost twenty years. He's built and sold two businesses and now runs a peer group, Vistage, while helping support his beautiful wife, Laura Pedersen, in her career as an opera singer.

One day, I overheard our friend Mary Alice Frank, president of the Northeast Ohio Red Cross, say something to Brad about a disaster run he'd made over the weekend. I asked Brad what she was referring to, and he said that he's a member of a Disaster Action Team.

It turns out that Brad volunteers to race to Red Cross headquarters when called upon, often in the middle of the night, to join a team of volunteers that goes to the sites of fires or other local disasters to provide relief. The team hands out blankets, food, and toiletries, and finds a place for displaced families to stay. Oftentimes, according to Brad, they just need to sit quietly with the victims as they fight through the reality of their situation.

There are two things that strike me about Brad's work: I would never, ever allow anyone to wake me from a sound sleep in the middle of the night in my safe, warm home to race off into the night, and . . . unlike Joe, Brad doesn't get paid.

Why does he do it?

"You'd be surprised how good I feel when I get home early that morning, Tim, like I just did something really meaningful for someone who can never repay me."

E-Hip-Hop

Howard Washington is twenty-something years old and was our foundation's first intern back in 2008.

He grew up in West Akron in a rough neighborhood. There were problems in his family and things never quite settled in the fifteen places he lived from his birth until he left at eighteen. But he had a tough mom who helped him and his brother and sisters make it through. In Howard's case, he was one of those lucky few whose basketball skills got him a scholarship to a local college.

There are a lot of unusual things about Howard. One is his degree, a bachelor of fine arts in dance, which he earned while also starring as point guard on the school's team.

Another is Howard's unwavering belief that hip-hop dance should surpass sports as a way for his community to break out of the claws of poverty. His simple theory is based on his own observations: (1) more people can do it, (2) it teaches young people respect for their bodies, (3) it encourages pride in cultural heritage, and (4) fitness sharpens the mind.

To try out his philosophy, Howard created a pilot program

for one of our charter school partners, making hip-hop the primary activity in their physical education program. Since the school is known as E-Prep, he named his team "E-Hip-Hop."

After graduating from college, Howard became E-Prep's full-time physical education teacher, and this fall, Howard will become principal of Northeast Ohio College Preparatory School. Howard is one of my heroes because he inspires hundreds of kids with otherwise bleak futures to transform themselves just as he did.

Oh, and Howard still teaches hip-hop most nights of the week and on the weekends as well—mostly without pay.

A Rich Hero I've Never Met

Warren Buffet is no more a saint than Joe, Brad, or Howard, but he too is becoming a service hero to me due to what's known as the "Buffet–Gates Pledge," launched in 2010.

As of this writing, Buffett has led 114 billionaires to agree, irrevocably, to give most of their fortunes to charitable causes. Over $250 billion will be invested towards making the world better because of Mr. Buffet's pledge idea. That makes him a hero in my mind, no matter what else he does.

Buffett, Howard, Brad, and Joe are just four of hundreds of heroes I've admired in recent years. But there are as many out there as I have time to work for. I don't have a billion dollars, so I can't get in on Buffett's pledge, and I don't have the constitution to ride on a dusty pickup truck or go out on disaster calls in the middle of the night, and I certainly can't hip-hop dance, but I do aspire to model my life after these lives of significance.

Walking the Walk

In Chapter 7, you met my hero, Father Norm, who left me with the real hero's secret to success.

Norm was standing in his priestly garb at the casket of a forty-seven-year-old woman whose husband was pleading with him. "Tell me why this happened," he begged. "Just tell me it's God's plan, Father, and maybe I will be able to handle this better."

"Roy," Norm said, "nothing our faith teaches us will resolve the pain you and I feel right now. So if I told you Judy died for a reason, I would be lying. I don't feel that way anymore than you do."

Then came the punch line, which I hope I'll never forget. "What I *can* say, Roy, in fact I promise you, is that I will walk with you every step of this painful journey."

Real heroes, to me, are not supermen or superwomen. They do not leap tall buildings or do things no mortal person can do. They are regular people with a gift—in this case the gift was simply being able to be present for someone in need.

• • •

Graceful presence is difficult for me to achieve. I'm anxious by nature and often my help is actually a means to gain control over another human being. My mom often warned me when she noticed me "lording over" a friend or a sibling. My ego tends to get in the way of my loving spirit.

Like all people, I am insecure. I have a deep need to be loved; I crave it. And often that craving, matched with a hearty dose of ego, leads me to do things that, looking back, are painful to remember. Recognizing that craving and the messes I've caused as a result of it does not make me bad or good; it makes me human. Recognizing my frailty is key to becoming authentic in service and getting out of my own way.

At the end of a long series of sessions, a psychotherapist once told me that my two most compelling characteristics were dominance and people-pleasing. "What does that mean?" I asked.

"You want people to do what you tell them to do," she said, "then thank you for it."

"How do you interpret that?" I wanted to know.

"You are eternally screwed," she said.

A woman named Brené Brown, who has studied shame and vulnerability, gave a wonderful TED Talk in 2012. Her research indicates that most of us are trapped in a cycle of avoiding our shame and denying our vulnerability. Her findings reveal that, counterintuitively, it is only through embracing our vulnerabilities and imperfections that we can engage in our lives from a place of authenticity and worthiness. And it is through finding our worthiness that we become more empathetic.

I've learned to forgive my own faults partly by remembering the title of an album from the 1960s by The Firesign Theater: *I Think We're All Bozos on This Bus*. I think we are, indeed, all bozos—*and all heroes*—on this bus of life, and so I frequently try to remind myself, my friends, and my partners of this fact.

We will make good moves and bad ones, and we will have good days and bad ones. And the heroes in my life have plenty of both.

CHAPTER 9

Helper's High

Charity is really self-interest masquerading under the form of altruism. . . . I give myself the pleasure of pleasing others.
—Anthony de Mello

FOR YEARS IT seemed debatable whether smoking caused cancer and heart disease. Now there is no uncertainty. Similarly, traditional medical science still seems ambivalent about the connection between our minds and bodies and whether our mental state affects our physical well-being. But someday I trust that the theory of a mind–body connection will be a universally accepted truth.

Medical and psychiatric research is slowly but surely clearing up the debate over the mind's connection to the body. It took fifty years of research and debate to get warnings on cigarette packs, so in my lifetime I probably won't witness the ultimate scientific certainty that the mind connects to body. It's even less likely that wealth-seeking's connection to anhedonia will be confirmed in my lifetime. Still, the early adapters will find a better way of living as surely as early quitters were less likely to get lung cancer.

I'm not a scientist, so my assertions in the next few paragraphs (and throughout this book) are products of a few weeks of searching through references found via Wikipedia and Google. What I read revealed that psychological studies supporting the concepts in this book are plentiful, if not yet fully established.

One citation I found on Wikipedia identifies a phenomenon called "helpers' high." Researchers observed that after performing a kind act, people first experience a moment of euphoria then settle into a longer-lasting state of calmness. What's going on chemically when we do good things is our bodies releasing endorphins that produce the physical sensation of calm. The subsequent, longer-lasting improvements to one's sense of self-worth reduce stress, which in turn improves the general health of the helper, as stress is linked to such physical ailments as digestive disorders, sleep disturbances, and lethargy.

What it boils down to is that helping others is good for us, and that's why I give it so much credence in terms of building a happier, more satisfying life. Let's take a look at some of the evidence to support the theory.

The Science Says...

The Social Capital Community Benchmark Survey included thirty thousand interviews completed in two waves by researchers at the John F. Kennedy School of Government at Harvard University. Among other findings, the study states, "Those who gave contributions of time or money were 42 percent more likely to be happy than those who didn't give."

A literature review of philanthropic motivation studies done by Rene Bekkers and Pamala Wiepking in 2010 provides more evidence that helping others produces psychological benefits for the helper, also labeled "empathic joy."

In 1989, James Andreoni offered economic models of philanthropy that label this psychological value as "warm glow" or "the joy of giving." Most interesting to me is that Andreoni's search was borne of his belief that most giving is not a pure form of altruism.

Lastly, a massive study was done by Daniel Kahneman and published through the National Academy of Sciences in August of 2010. Kahneman's research tells us that well-being involves two separate aspects. First there is emotional well-being, or the emotional quality of an individual's everyday experience and how frequently he or she experiences feelings of happiness, sadness, anger, stress, affection, and so on, which adds up to whether or not he or she experiences life as pleasant or unpleasant the majority of the time. And second there is "life evaluation," which refers to the thoughts that people have about their lives when they think about them.

Kahneman specifically sought to discover whether, in terms of these two measures of well-being, people had found that money buys happiness. He learned that "when plotted against log income, life evaluation rises steadily. Emotional well-being also rises with log income, but there is no further progress beyond an annual income of $75,000." While people with low incomes experience more emotional pain and are statistically associated with such misfortunes as divorce, ill health, and being alone, people with high incomes did not necessarily experience relatively greater levels of happiness. As Kahneman writes, "We conclude that high income buys life satisfaction but not happiness, and that low income is associated both with low life evaluation and low emotional well-being."

If you're interested in reading more and don't mind a little jargon, you can find a flood of studies and information at www.sagepub.com, a publisher of scholarly works on the leading edge of social psychological and personality science.

Findings from the little research and reading I've done confirm for me that, beyond a certain income, money does not buy happiness, and helping others adds to physical and psycho-logical health. But research is secondary to me; life experience is always my primary teacher.

Sleep Is Good, But It's Not Mindfulness

My journey to believing that my mind affects my health required more than research. In the mid-1990s, I began reading books written by and attending retreats conducted by Jon Kabat-Zinn, founder of the Center for Mindfulness in Medicine at the University of Massachusetts Medical School. Kabat-Zinn and the current center director, Saki Santorelli, have published many books and scientific articles, but my favorite for beginning mindfulness practitioners remains Kabat-Zinn's first book, *Full Catastrophe Living*.

The specific practice I follow is *Vipassana*, originally a Buddhist discipline also known as "bare attention." Through weekly meetings, called *sangas*, with other practitioners and the daily practice of meditation and noble silence, I learned to notice my emotions and therefore reduce my stress-induced reactions. More closely connecting my mind and body helps me become more empathetic, which in turn produces helper's high.

I've practiced mindfulness meditation and loving kindness (*metta*) for almost twenty years. There is no chanting, singing, dancing, or praying in my practice; there is only sitting and noticing my breath. Twenty minutes sitting in the same relaxed but alert position allows my mind and body to quiet and become still. It might sound difficult—and it is—but the purpose of every sitting is to notice how unquiet our minds and bodies generally are. And through the simple act of noticing that, I can acquire the skills to deal more effectively with my racing mind.

My wife and I provide extremes of what this practice can do. Once when she joined me for a sanga, our teacher asked Alice how she felt during the meditation, and she said, "I slept. Is that good?"

My teacher said, "Oh, yes, Alice, sleep is very good—but it's not mindfulness!" Among other things, Alice is by nature the most mindful, empathetic person I've ever known.

Most beginners are more like me than Alice. For months, I constantly fidgeted, and my mind flew all over the place. Often frustrated after sitting, I'd say to my teacher, Paul, "This is horrible. I can't sit still!"

Paul would smile knowingly and say, "Yes, but you got through it, and you noticed that you weren't peaceful. That's the first step."

The ultimate goal of Vipassana and most Buddhist practices is to learn "loving kindness." The Buddha and the millions who've practiced mindfulness over the last 2,500 years believe that in settling our minds, we learn compassion and non-judgment of others.

My current teacher, John, wrote to me recently. "I have found that living in compassion, generosity, and wisdom are the answer for me," he said. "Not that I am there all the time—not by a long shot—but that at my deepest core, I know these truths and they are always available for me."

My "When" Existence

The difference between today and when I was younger is that I no longer sacrifice much to live the way I've chosen. My early life was spent living a "when" existence. Maybe this sounds familiar:

When I get married . . .
When I have a better job . . .
When I've accumulated enough savings . . .
When my kids are grown and gone . . .
When I retire . . .
. . . I'll serve others and be happy.

But it was hard to be happy while waiting for something better. My updated "when" could be when my children's careers take hold or when the foundation (or this book!)

succeeds…I'll be happy. But I've learned that if I live in this moment, I experience life more fully. I get to this moment by practicing mindfulness. And this moment is made better if I'm helping someone.

My Terminal Teacher

Most people don't seek service naturally, and I was no different. In fact, my earliest experiences in living a life of compassion were pretty clumsy. Often I'd find myself "helping" someone with a sense of urgency and control. My sister Sheila once told my mom, "Tim is at his worst when he is trying to be his best." Said differently, she had noticed that I only made the situation worse, not better, when I worked on others before working on myself.

My best teacher for healing myself, not others, was Mary Janice McCoy McCarthy, my brother Terry's wife. Jan became bed-ridden with cancer in 1985. I was thirty-three years old when she became disabled, and early on in her illness Terry asked me to stay with her one Saturday night. I was petrified and of course my worries were not about Jan; they were about *me*.

Take care of her? What would I even say to her? What do you do with someone who is terminally ill? I didn't know.

Jan was a true friend to me ever since she began dating Terry in the 1960s. It should have been natural for me to visit her, but I sweated bullets. I prepared endlessly: songs to entertain her, a planned menu, and the company of Alice and my kids for courage. Then the one-hour ride to her house seemed too short. I was scared to death that I would say or do something wrong.

I entered the house more or less on tiptoe. Jan's hospital-style bed was located in the area that used to be the dining room, which separated the kitchen from the living room, giving her a good view of both. In fact, her perch was set so that little could escape her view.

Jan was a very pretty woman, and while her illness had not diminished her looks, the first thing I noticed was that her face was pale and she had already lost quite a bit of weight. The doctors gave her around two years to live, which was about average for the rare form of sarcoma she had contracted near her spine. The pain that could arise from the small of her back, near all those nerves, was unimaginable to me. She seemed to be sleeping when I entered, and I was so nervous that I wondered if I was going to throw up.

Then she saw us. She lifted her torso up with the trapeze bar that hung over her bed and gave us a broad and peaceful grin. She beckoned our youngest, Caitlin, to climb up on the bed with her and have a chat while she suggested I get to making dinner.

All five of us seemed to exhale at once. With Jan, my worries were silly. One of her most amazing gifts was making everyone feel at ease, and that hadn't changed a bit. We talked and laughed and sang and ate and had as good a Saturday night as we'd ever had together.

We visited Jan every chance we got. We did home masses, birthday parties, holiday meals, and drive-bys on our way home from somewhere else. And we always left with more joy and courage than we arrived with.

In Jan's case, I suppose it was helper's high that made me feel such joy around her—but it was also something else. The inspiration of seeing someone so challenged and yet so relatively happy, loving, and peaceful changed our lives. Whether I visited alone or with Alice and the kids, I never drove away from Jan's house without feeling like I'd received far more than I'd given. I learned a ton about giving from Jan, and also that hope is a precious commodity.

More Proof of the Mind–Body Connection

During her illness, Jan further demonstrated that our minds are connected to our bodies. In 1985, when the doctors told Jan she'd live one to four years at best, she said, "I'm going to see my youngest child graduate from high school in 1995." Her words didn't sound like hope; they sounded like a decision. What followed was the most amazing demonstration of mind over matter I will ever witness. Jan did indeed attend her son Danny's graduation from St. Ignatius High School. She also went to the family celebration dinner afterward at a fancy restaurant, and a few months later, saw the youngest of her four kids off to college.

Less than a year later, satisfied her work was done and certain she was headed to a better place, Jan passed and left the hundreds of people at her funeral (she called it her "homecoming") better for having known her.

A Master of Disguise

Another time I remember sweating bullets while contemplating service to others was when I started going into the inner city in 1997. Again, it was all about *me*.

To attend my first meeting in the tough St. Clair–Superior neighborhood, I borrowed a neighbor's beat-up car so my nice car wouldn't look so obvious . . . or get stolen. I wore the oldest clothes I owned, ones I would wear if I were painting or working in the yard. And I worked myself into a frenzy wondering what I might find in such a tough neighborhood, particularly at night.

Here is what I found: very poor people who were very happy that we were working with them to serve their neighbors more effectively.

In a word, I found inspiration.

How could people with so little be so relatively happy and so interested in serving those less fortunate than themselves? How could I be so relatively fortunate but so relatively unhappy?

Over the next ten years, I was in this same neighborhood

at least once a week, and I never worried about anything except enjoying my teammates in service. They remain the most authentic people I know.

Cleveland's Poor Are Wealthy

You've already met Joe Cistone, the guy who said, "This is where I belong" in the poverty-stricken urban slums of El Salvador—and one of my personal heroes. The foundation's work in the 2000s also took us to the ghettos of Kenya and Naples, Italy, with Joe.

In Kenya, I met women whose genitalia had been mutilated in their youth so that their fathers could sell them for a cow to polygamous older men. I also met young women who had escaped their father's plans and were taught and cared for by older women who had experienced the same tragedy. In rural Kenya, we visited hundreds of orphans of AIDS victims who were settled into camps where they learned to farm well enough to become self-subsistent.

Near Naples, I met preteens who had been sold into sex slavery and were later rescued by Nigerian nuns who hid them and prepared them to return to mainstream society.

Without exception the people we met were hardy and joyful. At one evening meal, my family listened to the lead nun who travelled each day to the red-light district of Naples to await children who might decide to escape prostitution. I asked if she risked danger at the hands of the pimps who would lose money from these defections. She laughed. "Tim," she said, "We no fuss . . . We no fuss . . . We pray quietly. Then sometimes, every once in a while, a child comes and asks us what we are doing. We tell them quietly and invite them to safety, but Tim, we no fuss."

On our first mission trip to El Salvador, we were greeted by a Jesuit priest, Dean Brackley, who told us, "Your heart will be broken by what you see here, but it will be pieced back together in a way that will change you forever."

It was during the El Salvador trip that one of my most embarrassing moments occurred. On our very last day in the country, we visited the site of a massacre of women and children that occurred during the country's civil war. Standing in the field praying was a moving experience. With my head bowed, I had barely noticed a girl of nine or ten years old who had moved next to me and put her hand in mine. I looked down to see a barefoot, dirty, and barely clothed local who was lovely in her quiet presence.

I folded some money into her hand, excused myself, and ran back to the bus that had brought us to the site. Once alone and away from our group, I wept uncontrollably. Sometime later, the group came back and I kept my head down and, God bless them, no one ever mentioned this episode then or later.

The lesson to me was indelible: I was not fit, in ego or emotional makeup, to serve directly. A stronger person might have lovingly shared the moment with that young girl or even sat down to exchange quiet thoughts and encouragement with her. It still shames me to realize that I could not.

Today, I have very little direct contact with those we serve. No more bedside chats with Jan, visits to the inner city, or mission trips abroad. I've found my joy in service is more effectively deployed serving those who serve. I needed these experiences to become inspired, but it became evident to me that I would suffer compassion fatigue, a phenomenon I'll discuss in detail in the next chapter, more quickly than those better suited to directly serve. I also believe that with my current approach I can help people get farther, faster.

But the lessons from these experiences will never be forgotten. The very fact that every single service person I met, even in dire circumstances, had a sense of humor reminded me that there is abundance available for me in every moment. During several of the times Joe Cistone would notice me getting ready to cry, he'd lean over and say, "Can I get you a beer?"

Anthony de Mello's quote, which opened this chapter, says it all to me: "I serve myself when I serve others." And Father Dean was right: My heart has been changed forever. My heart will never be able to see someone wanting without considering what I might do to be helpful.

CHAPTER 10

Compassion Fatigue

We have all volunteered to be givers of light. In making
this effort, we are all going to burn.
—Viktor Frankl

OVER THE COURSE of this book, I've been asking the following
question: How do we surmount the anhedonia, addiction, and
despair so prevalent among Americans? For me, the antidote is
the helper's high that comes from mindful giving. But even this
gift comes with a cost.

Compassion fatigue, again from my research on Wikipedia,
is also known as secondary traumatic stress. It is a phenomenon
commonly found among people such as nurses, psychologists,
and first responders who work directly with trauma victims.
It boils down to gradual lessening of compassion over time—
becoming numb to the painful experiences of others.

It is a diagnosable psychiatric condition, and sufferers sometimes experience stress, anxiety, hopelessness, lessened capacity for pleasure, a negative outlook on life, and sleep disturbances. Whether a sufferer of compassion fatigue serves others as a volunteer or a professional, the condition can have detrimental effects on his or her work, including a decrease in productivity, an inability to focus, and the development of feelings of incompetency and self-doubt that were not present before.

As great as my helper's high can be, I will crash when I become compassion fatigued. The truth is that I don't really know if I've experienced diagnosable compassion fatigue. The only certainty is that overdoing it seems to wear me out, and sometimes even triggers my dysthymia.

In this chapter, I'll offer some stories and information to illustrate the dangers of compassion fatigue. When we give of ourselves, we must stress mindfulness, so that we don't burn through our resources unaware.

Help Gone Wrong

In the early 2000s, a family from war-torn Senegal, the Waleeds, who used the transitional housing project we supported, convinced me they needed substantial additional support, which I provided.

The Joseph House brought them into an apartment on our parish grounds and the wonderful volunteers at our parish worked to help the family obtain the things they would need to survive in the United States. Transportation, jobs, even training on simple skills, such as buying groceries, are often necessary for these transitions.

The Waleeds seemed exceptionally bright and ambitious and particularly loving to all who met them. They all had great smiles and seemed to live harmoniously as a family. Their accents were sometimes hard to understand, but they had a good command of English.

Soon after they arrived, their kids were all in schools and the mother and father were both working. They eventually rented a home in the neighborhood and seemed on their way to great things. We dreamed that someday they and all their children would gain degrees and realize their American dreams.

Then it all unraveled for me.

The patriarch of the family had estimated their living expenses, and I paid them from my own savings just to keep things simple. One Sunday, I was approached by one of the daughters, who told me that her sister had run away from home.

"Why in the world would she do that?" I asked.

With great struggle, almost terror in her eyes, she said, "It is not safe in our home."

I'll never know exactly what that meant, but it caused me to look more closely at things, and my findings were disappointing. The father was renting out rooms in his home to other refugees at a high cost. Along with collecting his children's wages and my unwitting support, he was building quite a savings.

In short, he was doing well financially and probably seriously misbehaving.

I felt sad and used. This would only be the first wave in my ongoing battle with compassion fatigue. In this and each subsequent battle, I've learned that it's okay to be vulnerable. I cannot help if I cannot be hurt. And those who help the least are those working from a platform of superiority and certainty.

But I also have learned to recognize that often people's words do not match their actions.

Misplaced Optimism

As I transitioned to serving those who serve the poor instead of direct service, I became intrigued by the work of a micro-lending organization in our area. I knew the director through a friend, and I jumped into backing the organization with both feet. I was sure this would be a better fit for me, since we would be supporting his organization instead of doing direct service—as I had done for the Waleeds.

After a couple years of quiet but substantial support, I agreed to accept an award from the micro-lender because I was convinced it would advance the cause. In fact, at the dinner in my honor, I announced a campaign that raised over sixty thousand dollars to lend to un-bankable businesses.

Soon after the dinner, as we became more connected with the organization, we realized that they had been operating for several years by borrowing from restricted funds. Without going too deeply into specifics, I'll say that it is unwise—if not illegal—for non-profit organizations to borrow from loan funds to pay operating expenses.

I was aghast. In fact, my first move to distance myself was to repay the sixty thousand dollars I'd raised from my friends.

The second thing I did was to question why the hell I was such an idiot. I remember one weekend actually thinking that perhaps I'd made the wrong choice in what to do with my life.

My purpose in sharing these embarrassing lessons with you is not just to prove I'm a bozo. It is to show the other side of helper's high. Encouraging others to give without being honest about the negatives would be harmful. Without temperance, giving can crush you.

Armed against Compassion Fatigue

As Frankl notes in the opening quote of this chapter, we are all "givers of light" who will resultantly "get burned." Feeling burned by the Waleeds and the micro-lender are just two of a dozen situations that wore me out. And there are many more individuals who were just using me to get money or some other form of support they needed who didn't deserve anyone's help. Over time, I've come to understand that's just how it goes; one must put their heart on the line to be of real service. There will always be fakers and fakers will always wear you out.

I've been asked how to avoid compassion fatigue and while there's no sure answer, here are a few things I've learned in my quest to be of service:

Lesson 1: Hold your compassion lightly and joyfully. Never take yourself too seriously. It's unlikely you will save the world any more than I will. But it is likely—no, it's guaranteed—that if you only do what you can and do it gladly, adjusting as you learn from your mistakes, life's moments of both joy and pain will be more fulfilling.

Lesson 2: Trust but verify. Since I made these errors, the good people I work with have helped create systems for evaluating our work to ensure that our services are well-placed and frequently reviewed. I'll discuss this in more detail in Chapter 12.

Lesson 3: Unless you are trained for it, leave the direct service in the hands of the professionals.

Compassion fatigue can be reduced by doing a fearless inventory of what we're good at and what we're not, verifying what we've been told and by remembering we will help but never solve this broken world.

Scars of Love

Dennis called me one Saturday afternoon last winter after finding his only child dead at twenty years old in his bed that morning. I remember being devastated by the news and wondering how such a thing could ever happen to such a man.

Dennis is a very compassionate man and an engaged listener. He spent important time with a young friend of mine who seemed close to suicide and has been very helpful to me during my own struggles. He's an MD and a degreed psychiatrist, so he's spent a lifetime listening to others during their most difficult times.

And so, during Dennis's overwhelming time of loss, I figured it was my turn to be bear up. In the days immediately following Gregory's death, Dennis broke down frequently into fits of sobbing, a few times uncontrollably. He ranted at length, both verbally and in print; really he wailed.

When it was time to give the eulogy at the funeral service, surely for the sake of his son, Dennis rose clear-eyed and strong-voiced and stood with his hand on the casket and said these words that I will never forget:

To love in this way is not easy. Love that is at the service of others leaves scars—scars of the heart and sometimes of the body. When you approach the stature of pure love you will understand. Such love is vulnerable; it may be taken advantage of, rejected, abused, and can be painful. Scars tell stories, both the wounding and the healing. The story of wounding is almost always a story of the lack of love. The story of healing is almost always a remarkable story of love. If you love you cannot avoid being scarred. If you love you cannot avoid being healed. The purpose of our lives is to love so that the creation may be made new.

Dennis's story is about tragedy, not compassion fatigue. But his words that day had everything to do with it. With true love, you will be scarred deeply—but you will also be healed. And creation will indeed be made new.

CHAPTER 11

How Much Is Enough?

*At a party given by a billionaire on Shelter Island, the late Kurt Vonnegut informs his pal, the author Joseph Heller, that their host, a hedge fund manager, had made more money in a single day than Heller had earned from his wildly popular novel **Catch 22** over its whole history. Heller responds, "Yes, but I have something he will never have." Vonnegut: "What in the world could that be?" to which Heller says, "I have enough."*
—John Bogle, *Enough*

THE UNITED STATES provides all its citizens unlimited earning potential. I am witness to the truth of that statement, having started only with my parents' example, a great education, and the five hundred dollars that was my share of their inheritance.

Now that my financial wealth is vast, the trick for me has been answering the question "How much does it take to make me happy?" This is a compelling question for me since the liquidity event because the happiest people I've met are rarely also the wealthiest.

But Without the Middle Class, We Won't Be Rich!

Almost 250 years into our great experiment, the United States finds itself in a funny place. Four hundred of our citizens make 20 percent of our annual income, while 43 million of us live below the poverty level. In the fifteen years prior to the great recession, those top four hundred people saw their income increase 392 percent and their average tax rate reduced by 37 percent. Since the great recession of 2007, the income disparity has worsened. The top 1 percent of earners gained 20 percent in wealth since then, while the other 99 percent rose 1 percent. The top 1 percent of Americans control 40 percent of all American wealth.

And while these statistics vary according to the studies I've read, it is not an overstatement to say America is becoming a somewhat feudal society (again). The distance from the richest to the poorest is its widest since 1928, and the trends indicate further widening of that gap in the short term. The Roaring Twenties, just prior to the Great Depression, were the last time that the rich were this rich and the poor this poor.

I've long since left the windmills to be tilted at by others. And my own place among the top 1 percent would put my tilting at risk of being called disingenuous. But it is my aim to find my place within existing societal norms, and so I have to question my life as it relates to this social phenomenon.

The bifurcation of wealth in the United States is much like the paradox of restaurant chain owners who believe they benefit from ignoring the health and well-being of their minimum wage employees. More than any other nation, the United States' wealth and productivity are driven by the middle class, the consuming public, and therefore the top 1 percent ultimately loses by hoarding just as surely as restaurant management loses by trimming ten cents off an hourly wage.

To me, this seems shortsighted at best, and mean-spirited at worst.

Enough for My Readers

As the wealth of the United States' 1 percent climbs steadily upwards, it's time to start asking, "How much is enough?" At what point do we have enough—not just to survive, but to feel truly satisfied, to feel like we don't need to keep adding to the pile?

I posed the following question to my blog readers: "How much is enough?" Their responses reveal great variations on the theme:

"Being able to donate $100,000 a year to charities I care about."

"Having the ability to take more risk at work."

"Knowing that today's needs are met and that tomorrow's are likely to be met. Needs, to me, are defined as safety, clean water, food, shelter, and healthy relationships."

"Being happy with who I am when I'm alone."

"Having enough to focus on fulfillment by giving, which is Carl Jung's fourth (out of four) stages of adulthood."

"Having enough to pay my bills and save a little."

"Having a thriving business that sustains my household and a few others, having the flexibility in my own schedule for spontaneous adventures, affording good care for my own health and my son's, and being comfortable in my own skin."

"Having freedom—not being tied down to things and people who wear you down, being able to be generous, and being able to go where you want."

"I've used food stamps and had my utilities shut off, and I worry constantly about making payroll for my employees, but in the end, adequate personal wealth is easy to attain here because it doesn't take much to live a good life in America."

"Yes, I'd like a boat, an updated bathroom, and a pool, but who really cares? I have love, food, and my kids, and we are safe and warm."

"I rarely think about it anymore because I was once quite wealthy and I lost it all. I was surprised because my life didn't change much after. In fact if it changed it was for the better. I'm having fun with what I'm doing now because of its purpose."

These responses reassured me that I cannot define for anyone how to be happy. The definition of "enough" follows the same rule as the definitions of happiness and significance: they are all inherently personal, situational, and perceptual. Striving to know our personal definitions can help us become more confident and peaceful, but these definitions will never be "resolved." They will continue to evolve over the course of a lifetime. But a target never set is forever missed.

The $80 Million Billionaire

John Bogle, author of the book *Enough*, is himself a very wealthy man. But in his peer group of wealth fund managers, he's a pauper. Despite founding and, for forty years, running one of the most successful mutual funds in history, his current net worth is estimated at $80 million. Keep in mind this is in a category of money managers who pay themselves ten times that amount annually and have amassed billions.

One of my favorite quotes from Mr. Bogle's book sums it up:

> *It is character, not numbers, that make the world go 'round. How can we possibly measure the qualities of human existence that give our lives and careers meaning? How about grace, kindness, and integrity? What value do we put on passion, devotion, and trust? How much do cheerfulness, the lilt of a human voice, and a touch of pride add to our lives? Tell me, please, if you can, how to value friendship, cooperation, dedication, and spirit.*

I know in my soul, as Bogle does, that I have more than enough. And so I spend most of my days working to serve those who serve the poor, but I also enjoy every reasonable perquisite provided to me by forty years of discipline and hard work.

It's really that simple.

A form of this line of thought came to me while driving with the top down in our 2002 Ford Thunderbird on a sunny, seventy-five-degree February day in Orlando, Florida. My sister and brothers live there, and for four to six weeks each winter, Alice and I stay in the apartment above my sister's garage. I work in the mornings, and then enjoy the sunshine the rest of the day and my family in the evenings.

With my favorite tunes blaring through my iPhone and my mind drifting to the memory of a wonderful dinner with my family the night before, an overwhelming feeling of gratitude hit me. It is hard to describe though I suspect you've had similar feelings—I just felt lucky and thankful that that moment was so pleasurable. And it was then that I wondered, would I be any happier if this were a 2014 Porsche convertible and I was headed for my $5 million winter mansion overlooking the ocean?

The answer was no, of course, since a sunny day off in Florida among a loving family seems like plenty. Like Joseph Heller, I have enough.

The Buddha said, "Beware of the striving." And yet it is also said that his last words on Earth were, "Strive on." This is a paradox that has been studied by scholars and Buddhist monks for years, and the conclusion most seem to come to is that the Buddha was modeling that there is a middle ground in every endeavor.

When we feel ourselves reaching for more and more and more, when we feel that we never have enough, we are certainly not satisfied. But most of us also won't live a happy life by renouncing all material goods and walking barefoot through the world. There is a middle ground, a place where we put forth enough effort and talent, and where we do, in fact, strive, but we do not feel chased by a constant need to attain, accomplish, and gain.

In the Chabad sect of Judaism, they teach a concept called "tzibur," the Hebrew word for "community." Breaking the word "tzibur" into its component consonants reveals that it is basically an acronym for three words: *tz* stands for *tzaddik*, or "holy person," *b* stands for *beinoni* or "the man in the middle," and *r* stands for *rasha* or "villain." Most of us will never be 100 percent righteous or 100 percent evil. We can relieve ourselves from the pressure to be the one and the fear of becoming the other. It's okay to be the middle guy. It's okay to reach for the middle.

Reaching for the middle means is that there is a place of satisfaction and acceptance outside of constant striving—outside of society's insistence that we "aim for the top." And most of us won't find this place in material goods. When I feel myself wanting the Porsche instead of the Ford, what is really behind that striving? I'll only end up disappointed by it. The next month I'll wish it were a Mercedes. So what makes me feel truly whole? When Alice is riding beside me in the car, whatever make or model it is.

It's not the material things that matter most to me; it's my relationships with other people. To a certain degree, owning things actually reduces the joy we can take in them. If I owned the Porsche, I'd be saddled with a fifteen hundred dollar monthly payment. I'd have to worry about where to park it safely. I'd have to make sure it stayed clean and maintained. And then I might feel guilty that I wasn't getting the maximum value out of it by using it enough. Ownership, ultimately, is a burden.

I remember once when I was a kid that I asked my dad why he quit smoking when many of his family members continued. "I hated being a slave to them," he said.

"What does that mean, Dad?" I asked.

"I never walked out of the house without making sure I had a lighter and my cigarette pack and an extra pack in case I ran out," he said. "I didn't want to be beholden to these objects anymore."

Sometimes wanting to own more and more makes us beholden. We think it will free us from our feeling of not having enough, when really it only buries us deeper.

I've saved my favorite reader response to the question of "How much is enough?" for last.

Most interestingly, the friend who wrote the following is extremely wealthy: "This is 'adequate wealth' to me: I want to live right now in gratitude and appreciation, allowing my wealth in all its forms to flow through me."

Enough for me is whatever I have—so that my life will not endlessly spiral toward my next unfulfilled desire.

CHAPTER 12

My Giving Pledge

The way I got the message out was to get a copy of Forbes, look down that 400 list, and start making phone calls! Bill and Melinda [Gates] did the same thing. So keep publishing the list so I can milk it.

—Warren Buffett, on how he and Gates have recruited
over one hundred billionaires to donate more
than half their wealth to charity

VERY FEW WILL ever receive the call for the Buffett–Gates Giving Pledge. In what I consider to be a heroic act (remember, my heroes are not saints), Buffet and Gates have created a campaign that could raise as much as a trillion dollars, all to be invested in charitable works. That would be about half what the United States government has spent on foreign aid over the last fifty years!

My personal giving pledge is very different, and yet it is no less sincere. It is the practice of mindful giving. In this chapter, I'll share with you the specifics of what my charitable giving looks like—not because these need be your specifics, but because the examples might help you on your path, and help you avoid some common pitfalls.

Distributing My "Abundance"

In the first two years after my ship came in, I gave away as much as I could as fast as I could. But it soon became clear that we would exhaust the foundation's resources in as little as ten years. That seemed incongruous with our primary goal of teaching others to build and sustain great missions.

In our third year, we created a sustainable platform to carry the foundation, hopefully for another generation or more. Here's how that works.

In January of each year, we add up the income on the foundation's marketable securities investments, plus the pre-tax profits from the monies in our direct business investments we have, including a restaurant company, media company, loan company, whiskey company, and about a dozen other ventures.

From the "net cash flow" generated the prior year, we subtract our business expenses, taxes, and personal expenses. The remaining money becomes the budget for the foundation for the following year. Let's say at the end of 2012 we had a $2 million total cash flow from all our for-profit ventures. So we take that $2 million and subtract the $1 million in business, tax, and personal expenses. The result of these calculations would be a 2013 foundation budget of about $1 million.

Simple and sustainable is our goal, and this appears to be a formula that could allow the foundation to carry on indefinitely.

"Profitable" Non-Profits

We also now use a simple, sustainable template for our non-profit investments. This "system" includes seven filters that prospective partners must get through to become fully engaged with us. The first filter, to assure we are not "all things to all people," is that the prospective partner must exclusively serve the poor. The second filter requires that the organizations we work with serve the poor sustainably. We currently see three long-term cures for breaking the poverty cycle: employment, entrepreneurship, and education. Here again the purpose of the filter is to focus on sustainability rather than just "giving."

But we learned our most interesting filter the hard way, and in fact it still takes about a year of working with an organization to gauge. It is "coach-ability." Well-intended people are not always coachable. But this of course is tricky, since un-coachable people don't see themselves as un-coachable.

The soul of our work is discipline. We never engage in decision-making with a partner, but we do require disciplined decision-making. Those already convinced of their decision-making skills usually chafe at being coached.

The other hard-to-discern filter is collaborative spirit. Like many growing "industries," there is much duplication in the non-profit world. In Northeast Ohio, for example, there are currently over six thousand non-profits. Pick a category of service and a search will produce dozens of groups with similar purposes. Because of this, we find organizations that welcome working with other similar-minded organizations can scale projects more efficiently and effectively. Sadly, the majority of non-profits operate with a "not invented here" attitude and strictly fly solo.

Our process or system with every significant partner takes five years and is shaped like a bell curve. Early on, our investments of time and money build slowly and then peak at year three. We wind down our investments as the organization shows that they've got the hang of it. It's been hard to say goodbye to a few of the great ones we've supported, but we are committed to sustainable practices. Said simply, if our work has been good it should be done by then, and if we have not been successful, that's another reason to move on!

$2.3 Trillion for What?

We generally "finish building airplanes while we're flying them." Our giving plans have required us to deal with the polarity of being both flexible and firm. Innovation requires us to plan while searching.

Planning is important. Thorough yet concise written planning is not negotiable in our organization. Without a plan, there is no basis for allocating resources and no way to measure progress.

But we must at the same time "search."

William Easterly's influential book *The White Man's Burden* led me to appreciate this term. He uses it to explain why the West has spent $2.3 trillion over the last fifty years in foreign aid, and yet only a small portion of that huge investment has been effective in eliminating poverty while brandishing our reputation. Our impact on poverty is uncertain, and many we've "helped" hate us.

Easterly's primary finding is that our approach has been to *plan* based on our own research and perceptions rather than to *search* for solutions with our underdeveloped partners. Planning without engaging those most affected by our plans creates failure while at the same time earning us a reputation of arrogance. Westerners are learning the hard way that plans funded and executed from a distance are, at best, well-intentioned but wasteful.

The ideas contained in Easterly's book are provocative and actionable:

> *A Planner thinks he already knows the answers; he thinks of poverty as a technical engineering problem that his answers will solve. A Searcher admits he doesn't know the answers in advance; he believes that poverty is a complicated tangle of political, social, historical, institutional, and technological factors. A Searcher hopes to find answers to individual problems only by trial-and-error experimentation. A Planner believes outsiders know enough to impose solutions.*

Easterly cites a case in Africa many years ago when a well-intentioned agency sent $5 million worth of mosquito nets to an African government to fight malaria. Most of these nets, however, found their way onto the black market to be re-sold and used for such things as fishing nets and wedding veils. The solution to this type of debacle, in Easterly's view, is to begin on the ground searching with locals for the right distribution network *before* we buy and ship the nets.

My challenges are simpler but no less intractable.

A Few Steps Forward

Now five years into the "new" foundation, we are making sub-stantial gains to support those who serve the poor:

Micro-lending: In northeast Ohio in 2014, there is just almost $10 million available in increments of $10,000–$100,000 for un-bankable entrepreneurs where there was no money available in 2010.

Mentoring non-traditional college students: This fall we will achieve over one thousand connections between first generation college students and people willing to support those students through a software platform developed in 2010 and revised by trial and error since then. Prior to this work, there was no existing mentor-ing program locally, and with another year of success, we will roll out the platform first in Ohio, then nationally.

Social enterprise incubator: Our third and final effort is to offer micro-lending and education for un-bank-able entrepreneurs with a social mission. Our third class will graduate spring of 2017.

The path to these developing success stories are littered with mistakes, but we've been fortunate to have the resources and collaborators to suffer many setbacks and still find the footing to take many steps forward. I share these good works only as proof that doing good can be done with a vengeance.

The Search for My Giving Pledge

Plans have a beginning and end; searches do not. Even the best plans require lots of adjustments. My "giving pledge" is just such a search. Another very wealthy hero of mine, Stewart Kohl, once told me, "We are, at all times, in either a vicious or a virtuous cycle." Stewart's point is that a good journey drives us to continually improve our approach while accepting that there is no giving destination. How could I ever know how the world will evolve over the rest of my lifetime, let alone over the lifetimes of succeeding generations who might use The Business of Good as their commitment to social change and innovation?

But whatever my or your giving pledge becomes, it is to me the antidote to anhedonia. It is the alternative to a purposeless pursuit of pleasure from material goods and the continual failure to obtain it.

Wealth Is Ignoble

America's free public library system, the buildings in which generations have found betterment through knowledge, is inextricably connected to Andrew Carnegie. Over twenty-five hundred public libraries were constructed under Carnegie's giving concept. To any town willing to sustain a free library with public funds, his foundation provided the land, building, and original inventory of books.

Mr. Carnegie built his fortune creating what became the United States Steel Corporation when he sold Carnegie Steel to J.P. Morgan for 1901's equivalent of $13.5 billion. His concept of philanthropy, however, was already well developed and is best described in his 1889 article now known as "The Gospel of Wealth." The fundamental concept Carnegie promoted is that the wealthy can attain a greater good by sharing their surplus as effectively as they built that surplus.

In the document, he says, "In the end, accumulation of wealth is ignoble in the extreme. I assume that you save and long for wealth only as a means of enabling you to better do some good in your day and generation. . . . There is no class so pitiably wretched as that which possesses money and nothing else."

Carnegie lived well, just as I do. But he ardently believed that inherited wealth is unproductive and he used centuries of monarchy in Europe as proof of his point. In another part of his article, Carnegie wrote, "Surplus wealth is a sacred trust which its possessor is bound to administer in their lifetime for the good of their community."

When this book was first conceived, I intended to share a template for those who want to grow by giving from their own excess wealth, whatever the amount. But during its writing I came to realize that *any* approach we choose to share our excess wealth is a good one, and an individual's wealth is not simply limited to money. There are many other forms of wealth such as time, knowledge, love, and kindness. And because any giving pledge leads to a virtuous cycle—a life of giving, loving, and living more fully—I encourage you to create your own pledge to help others with the form of wealth you have in abundance.

CHAPTER 13

On Higher Ground

Up to a point a man's life is shaped by environment,
heredity, and movements and changes in the world about
him; then there comes a time when it lies within his
grasp to shape the clay of his life into the sort of thing he
wishes to be. Only the weak blame parents, their race,
their times, lack of good fortune, or the quirks of fate.
Everyone has it within his power to say this: **I am today;**
that I will be tomorrow.
—Louis L'Amour, *Education of a Wandering Man*

WE ALL SHARE the fact and fate that life is temporary. If this book
has met its goal, you are convinced that while we are here we
can make a difference.

The size of that difference is irrelevant, as is expressed by
the old fable about the boy throwing starfish from the shore

back into the sea before they died. The old man said, "Son, face it, you can't save these thousands of starfish each wave is throwing to shore." To which the boy responded, "Yes, but I can save this one," as he threw another back into the water.

It's good to measure progress based on one's impact, especially when we are blessed with so much to give. This leads to continual improvement and perhaps more "starfish" being saved. But mindful giving requires that I always think like the fabled little boy, realizing that each attempt at a good deed is enough.

A Progressively Better View

I believe the end is in the means. That is, you can have a lot more fun trying to make a positive difference in others' lives than living in empty abundance.

It's been said that you can't take a helicopter to the summit, but that was before financial engineering and inherited wealth came along. Trust-babies, CEOs, and hedge fund managers can now buy the helicopter and fly it to the peak, or turn the mountain into a helipad.

For me, that misses the point, which of course is the journey. My journey to the life I dreamed of living has been slow and meandering at times, but that slow growth and progress has been my reward.

I've slipped going up the mountain as many times as I've gained traction. Getting a few hundred feet up the mountain happens on a good day, and I still have many days where it seems I'm sliding back a thousand feet.

Perhaps the punch line is that there is no summit—just always better views as we climb higher.

Slipping Back Down the Mountain

During the three years immediately following our for-profit success, I spent an unsustainable amount of money on charitable endeavors that I still find hard to justify. To carry the analogy, I took a long slide back down the mountain of my dreams. Looking back, here's why that happened: I put people and positions ahead of strategy. I figured foundations first need a strong executive director, so I hired an excellent one who in turn built a strong staff.

Sadly, what I really needed first was a business plan. But strangely, I didn't remember that fact, even after years of following a "business plan first" method of doing business. Within a couple years, it had become a mess for everyone involved, something I still regret.

New philanthropists believe choosing a cause and putting money behind that effort will cure a problem. It doesn't, and it certainly didn't for me. I was once lamenting this fact to my friend, Sister Rita Mary Harwood, and she said to me, "Tim, if money were the answer, the Christians and Jews would have solved world poverty years ago!"

Climbing Back up the Mountain

In late 2009, I finally wrote a business plan for the foundation.

A business plan requires that you set goals first, then build strategies, and then build the organization that will support the goals and strategies. Structure and process first, then people.

When we began to implement the plan in 2010, The Business of Good had ten board members, six full-time staff members, and had spent $850,000. We spent five dollars on administration for every one that we donated.

In 2013, we invested about $1 million, and our ratio of administration to donations was one to five—a complete reversal from 2010.

We operate virtually, with one contract employee, our managing director, who contracts managers for projects. In the burgeoning non-profit sector, consultants abound, so finding good, committed managers on contract is doable.

Most importantly, our entrance and exit from organizations we support follows a disciplined process that we are continually refining. And we incessantly measure, allowing even for measurement's imperfections.

Let's say we promise to help a non-profit to reduce their revenue base from 50 percent fundraising to 20 percent by adding an earned income component. A great example is the International Partners in Mission "immersion trips" described in Chapter 8. Donors who wish to see the projects they support can, for a fee, travel with us to Central America, Africa, and South Asia to experience first-hand the work being done. Creating, selling, and managing immersion trips more than replaced income from unstable fundraising techniques. These trips also affected all other giving, since once donors have been immersed, they often become—as I am—dedicated to IPM for life.

Of course, it was a process that took years to refine and expand effectively and profitably, so we set goals and milestones to measure our progress. In this case, the work has been a remarkable success. In others, we fail to reach the goals—but it is only by looking at mileposts that we know if we are "talking" change or "walking" it.

I Know Half This Stuff Is Working, I Just Don't Know Which Half

I grew up in the advertising business so I am comfortable with ambiguity. Not everyone is, and yet the issue of "measurement" has become a lightning rod in the non-profit sector. The reason my background helps is that, as in advertising, one must *neither* measure everything *nor* measure nothing. In thirty-five years of advertising, perfect measurement eluded me (and all others who are honest about such things), and so I expect measuring non-profit success to be no different. The answer, as with most of life, is in the middle.

It's hard to measure as surely as a business would like, and yet it's unwise to give up measuring. So we coach new foundations to align with current efforts in their areas of interest, and we promote collaboration over invention.

Identifying a productive niche for our work was—and is—our overarching goal. What can we do that others are not already doing? It seems so far that collaborating to serve those who serve the poor by developing good business practices is that niche.

An emerging niche for us may also be aligning with socially conscious for-profit businesses, as the revenue could expand our own mission work. We currently have three fully functioning social businesses in our group and are targeting more.

For those willing to focus on continuous improvement, the road rises endlessly. And whether you become involved full-time, as I have, or you just want the good feeling of giving more, even the hard lessons are easier to take.

Business's Seat at the Table

When I went back to school for an MBA at Ohio State University's Fisher School of Business in 2005, one of the first lectures from Dr. Jay Dial included these words:

> *It is time for business to take a seat at the table of social change. It is obvious to me that government and non-*

government service organizations have not been able to fulfill our society's need for change. This is not to their detriment as they may be doing as well as they can do. It is to say that the discipline of business could enhance what is already being done and perhaps make it more effective over time. In any event, as community-based organizations, business can no longer "leave it to someone else."

It was a thought that never occurred to me. The life I'd lived building successful businesses could serve an even higher purpose? I was glad to sign up for that.

Currently, living wages for the working poor is a major issue in the United States. I don't advocate for either side emerging in the debate, as they both strike me as being comprised of just the same old sound bites. I realize the issue's polarity.

So, rather than lob verbal hand grenades over the political wall, business can and should get out in front of this and other social issues. If someone is willing to work, isn't that better for them and for our businesses, and more efficient than welfare? Broad legislation often has unintended consequences, so I would far prefer that business take a proactive, rather than reactive, stance on such chronic social problems.

Or, "take our seat at the table," as it were. Otherwise, business is just another victim.

Progress, Not Perfection

My early path toward building a traditional foundation did not guarantee that I would become effective at generating social change. In fact, it made it harder. Now the challenge is to continue to learn from my mistakes and come up with new plans and measurements of those plans so that I may effectively make the world a little bit better.

There is no destination, no simple formula, for the other-directed journey—no *Social Good for Dummies* book to follow.

Over time, I seek progress, never perfection, to find meaning in my life. It's not unlike maturing from childhood. That is, until you forgive your parents, realizing their humanity, it's hard to realize your own humanity and get on with growing up.

The first years of sliding down and climbing up this mountain of change have been nothing short of terrific. The view has significantly and continuously improved.

There is no doubt your journey to overcome anhedonia is and will be different. It's deeply personal. An elder priest friend, one of the most inspiring people I've known, wrote me recently with this thought:

I do not inspire others by intending to. I try instead just to focus on the person I am with and the moment I am in and react as naturally as I can to their thoughts. Usually,

*my history and persona have enough gravitas to hold their
attention and to make them feel encouraged. And usually,
most of the folks I am present to are thoughtful or they
would not have approached me, as the "means is the end."
People figure their own stuff out in my presence versus me
figuring it out for them or "inspiring" the facts of their
matters.*

That must be why my mother listened so quietly and well.

Perhaps you're starting at thirty or at seventy-five—and
perhaps you've served well or not at all.

It really doesn't matter because this is a journey unlike any
other, and focusing on a destination invites only frustration.
I've long since accepted that instead of changing The World,
there is much more meaning if I seek to change only My World
and how I relate to it.

And that takes a ton of pressure off!

If It's Not Fun, You're Doing It Wrong

Finally, since giving can be painful at first, here are a few points
to consider when developing your own plan.

Give from your surplus. It is generally believed that the
Bible says we should give until it hurts. The problem with that
idea is that it often leads to piety and judgment. There's no end
to my friends who are giving more than they should. And the

result in many cases is latent anger and frustration when things don't go as they planned. These martyrs often hurt others as much as they hurt themselves, which is sad since their intentions are usually good.

Small gifts—of time and treasure—count just as much as big ones. My sister Mary has never had an extra cent to share with others. She raised her family on her wits and very creative management of what little they had. But Mary is one of my models of giving because she gives time, a resource she has in greater quantity than money. She's worked thousands of hours at her church and school to help them put on fundraisers. And the most interesting part to me is that she always, and I mean always, does it with a smile and lots of energy. It's so much wiser and it also affects everyone involved in the causes she serves because her work not only raises money; it lifts spirits.

Give gladly. Mary's mark among her friends and co-workers is that they often wonder why she's so happy. My brother Steve, whom my mother called "the Great Samaritan," is the same way. He sings and teases while he's changing a tire for someone he found stranded on the side of the highway.

I remember often what Father Norm taught me: "It's not enough to give; Timmy, we must give gladly."

What Norm meant was that the non-profit world is already swarmed with people who are giving to get to heaven or to exercise power that they cannot achieve in their work world. What a shame, since bad attitudes drive away new volunteers and donors who see what's going on and avoid service.

To paraphrase Mom's "free hand" line: "If you can't give gladly, don't bother giving."

Beware the fakers. Like all newer businesses I've grown up with, those who may appear to be walking the walk are often just talking the talk. And many of them charge you for the privilege of listening to their noise.

For example, many in social enterprise, including myself early on, unwisely sell the idea that non-profits can fix their revenue problems by starting businesses—and yet it is rarely true. Thankfully, I have two good teachers in Rick Aubry and Nancy Osgood who showed me that very few non-profits should invest in developing earned income streams. And even the few who do invest should do so only after long and careful planning.

Celebrate your mistakes and forgive easily. By tradition, the non-profit world is an inefficient and frustrating world. Coming directly from a fully controlled corporate environment, my mistakes are frequent and in some cases, embarrassing.

I try to remember that mistakes are my teachers. I must make them, accept them, and then get over them. I will go farther faster by forgiving and forgetting than I will by judging myself or my colleagues.

There's an exchange in the movie *City Slickers* where Curly the cowboy tells Mitch the city slicker the secret of life. It goes like this:

CURLY: Do you know what the secret of life is?
[*Holds up one finger.*] This.
MITCH: Your finger?
CURLY: One thing. Just one thing. You stick to that and the rest don't mean shit.
MITCH: But, what is the "one thing?"
CURLY: [*Smiles*] That's what you have to find out.

Though it is often difficult and sometimes embarrassing, I'm having fun finding out what my "one thing" is. Maybe I'll find something better, but today, I'm following a path centered on serving others gladly. And each day I seem to have a little more fun doing so.

Always, We Begin Again

Music is a meaningful part of my life. I most enjoy the singer/songwriter poets. Early on I enjoyed Bob Dylan, Neil Young, Paul Simon, and later, David Wilcox, Amos Lee, and the Indigo Girls because they create music with meaning for me, songs I can reflect on.

My current favorite artists/poets are the Avett Brothers. The words from their song "February Seven" seem to summarize this book and spark my final thought.

There's no fortune at the end of the road
That has no end
There's no returning to the spoils
Once you've spoiled the thought of them
There's no falling back to sleep
Once you've wakened from the dream
Now I'm rested and I'm ready and I'm ready to begin.

The world is ready for you to begin on your path away from anhedonia and onto truly abundant living, whatever form it might take and whatever form of wealth you choose to share. I wish you untold happiness on the journey—and may you share your happiness and good fortune with many others.

Peace.

CPSIA information can be obtained
at www.ICGtesting.com
Printed in the USA
FFOW03n1528201216
30618FF